Nimrod: Awards 33

Nimrod International Journal

Awards 33
What Time Is It?

Nimrod International Journal IS INDEXED IN
HUMANITIES INTERNATIONAL COMPLETE

ISBN: 0-9794967-8-0   ISSN: 0029-053X
Volume 55, Number 1
Fall/Winter 2011

THE UNIVERSITY OF TULSA — TULSA, OKLAHOMA

This issue of Nimrod is dedicated to
Edwynne Krumme,
1923-2011

Inspiring teacher of French Literature and
Language at the University of Tulsa
and friend to all who think deeply
and know that politics and poetry can
and should speak the truth.

Once Again Time and Awards

Speaking of "time," its paradigm, palimpsest, recurrence: we must not forget that, once again, at this time of year, we celebrate the annual *Nimrod* Awards, a poetry and fiction competition and subsequent all-day writing conference that has gained prestige and a remarkable number of eager attendees over its 33-year history of awarding prizes. In this contest, *Nimrod*'s yearly event, we select finalists from over 1200 submissions from all over the country, and rely on our esteemed judges to make the even more difficult selections of winners in poetry and fiction from the finalist groups. Each manuscript received for this competition is scrupulously treated: At least two, and as the distinctions become more difficult, often as many as five editors lavish time on reading each submission in order to select the finalists in each category. The judges, this year Amy Bloom and Linda Pastan, make their selections of winners and honorable mentions from these finalists. The results, with which we are delighted, are presented for your enjoyment in this issue.

Acknowledgements

This issue of *Nimrod* is funded by donations, subscriptions, and sales. *Nimrod* and The University of Tulsa acknowledge with gratitude the many individuals and organizations that support *Nimrod*'s publication, annual prize, and outreach programs: *Nimrod*'s Advisory and Editorial Boards; and *Nimrod*'s Angels, Benefactors, Donors, and Patrons.

ANGEL ($1,000+)
Ellen Adelson, Margery Bird, Joan Flint, Stephani Franklin, Susan and Robert Mase, Randi and Fred Wightman, The John Steele Zink Foundation

BENEFACTOR ($500+)
Ivy and Joseph Dempsey, The Jean and Judith Pape Adams Foundation, Cynthia Gustavson, Bruce Kline, Ruth K. Nelson, Donna O'Rourke and Tom Twomey, Lisa Ransom and David Flesher, Ann Daniel Stone, Joy Whitman, Jane Wiseman

DONOR ($100+)
Helen and M. E. Arnold, Harvey Blumenthal, Richard Bryan, Mary Cantrell and Jason Brimer, Katherine Coyle, Harry Cramton, Jackie and Mark Darrah, Kimberly Doenges, Marion and William Elson, Nancy and Ray Feldman, Ken Fergeson, Sherri Goodall, Ann Graves, Helen Jo Hardwick, Ellen Hartman, Nancy Hermann, Robert James, Elizabeth and Sam Joyner, The Kerr Foundation, George and the late Edwynne Krumme, Robert LaFortune, Mary Lhevine and George Schnetzer, Roberta Marder, Geraldine McLoud, Rita Newman, Catherine Gammie Nielsen, Helen Beth and Johnie O'Neal, Nancy and Thomas Payne, Pamela Pearce, Katie and Ron Petrikin, Judy and Rodger Randle, Marcialyn and Bernard Robinowitz, Patricia Rohleder, Margaret Schula, Joan Seay, Diane Seebass, Frances and Bruce Tibbetts, Dorothy and Michael Tramontana, Ann Watson, Marlene and John Wetzel, Melissa and Mark Weiss, Penny Williams, Josephine Winter, Mary Young and Joseph Gierek, The Thomas Young Trust, Rachel Zebrowski, Ann Zoller

PATRON ($50+)
Margaret Audrain, Kay and Daniel Duffy, Sue and William Flynn, Linda and Marc Frazier, Martha King-Clark and Stephen Clark, Simon Levit, Maria Lyda, Olivia Marino, Samanthia and Andrew Marshall, Carolyn Sue Stees, Krista and John Waldron, Peter Walter, Michelle and Clark Wiens, Ruth Weston, Martin Wing, Douglas Young

TABLE OF CONTENTS

FRANCINE RINGOLD

Editor's Note
Nimrod: What Time Is It?

Though it might seem unbelievable to those who know me, when I was a little girl, probably eight or nine, I was very shy. My grandmother tried to break me of my timidity by urging me, under her watchful eye, to go up to strangers in the park or on a busy street in New York City where we lived and ask: "Could you please tell me the time?" So perhaps it's inevitable for me to be editing an issue that attempts, among other things, to deal, once again, with the question of time.

Often *Nimrod* announces a theme that we hope will ignite the imagination of the best writers who are always just "out there" awaiting the spark that will bring together the various and multiple gifts that are milling about, looking for a center, a focus. However, as is the case with this issue filled with *Nimrod* Award winners, finalists, and poems and stories accepted over-the-transom during the year, there are times when a theme erupts from the material we have accepted purely on the basis of quality. So it is, once again, with "Time."

Perhaps this should not surprise us; the nature of time has been one of the central issues of contemporary physicists, philosophers, historians, archeologists, poets and prose writers. The preoccupation with time seems to be always with us, young and older, not only as a chronological, linear marking but as a palimpsest, a ghost-writing of the layers of experience that enter each moment we truly live and not just exist. Salvador Dali's 1931 painting "The Persistence of Memory," depicting what appears to be a melting clock, is the visual image that most clearly symbolizes shifting concepts of time. From the early part of the twentieth century, we remember also the stylistic experiments of Proust, Joyce, Woolf, Faulkner, and the science fiction writers who wrote of space-time travel before the scientists confirmed their imaginative discoveries. That preoccupation seems to have surfaced again—at this time.

The writers represented here seem to be asking: Why not? Why not once again, after almost 100 years, revisit that preoccupation with time? For each moment we breathe, think, speak, write, remember—we are in time and out of time. We are reveling in that transitory space where we reshape, move freely from time past to time present, to time future, while inhabiting the present moment, that "spot of time," that is, as Bergson said, "real time" where past, present, and future interact.

In this issue, we search in multiple and various ways for the answer to "What time is it?" Some speak as if we could differentiate, as if chronological, linear time actually marks off minutes, hours, days in order to usefully measure the everyday affairs of life—as if we could know where we have been and where we are going. Some reflect on time's relativity and its mystery, just as the Australian Aborigines speak of "the dream time" from which all life emerges. Theories, beliefs, elegant equations, like life itself, are circular. They satisfy for a time; then they are replaced or at least altered, each time leaving the ghost of past theories and the promise of future speculations.

For example, in this issue of *Nimrod*, the first-prize award-winning achievement of Hayden Saunier is a linked sonnet sequence that not only echoes traditional forms of the past but correspondingly deals, in the repetitions and intricacies of its complex development, with how the "past keeps changing," how "the past requires several mirrors angled backward," in order to accommodate all that is "gaining on us," all that comes up faster than the eye can see.

"Shadowed: Unheard Voices," an experimental series in which poets respond to old photos, finding their own lives in those of others, enlivens the past, makes it a montage of the present.

Suzanne Cleary's second-prize-winning poem, "Amazing", confronts the irony of split-second timing: if Patty had sat in her car five minutes longer in clock time, she would have been struck by a meteor, become another nightmare on Elm Street. In finalist Mary B. Moore's "Drinking the Gin of Time," space and time are a cartographer's dream and a daughter's silent engine, time-slurred, breeding tears from trees, while in Brent Pallas's poem "My Dear Emma," one is thankful that "in such a messy world" time is marked by "late afternoon light." Yet occasionally, time stands almost still. It is a "lull" in Katie Kingston's "Woman Resting," a "drift beneath the white portal into a white dream." Sarah Wetzel's "Explaining God to Israeli Children" suggests that "space and time," like God, are a means of measure, and with Spinoza and Pythagoras, the poem ends in an ironic nod to the existence of all that is unknowable.

Then there are the poems and stories that deal with "doing time," such as Clark Knowles's "Trephine," in which Jolie, an ex-con, with a timeless and immeasurable hunger, is on a doomed march, absent any future beyond the next McDonald's. If Jolie's past is in part attributable to genetics, as suggested in Patricia Hawley's "Transmutation," and James Meetze's "Phantom Hour," time may be unredeemable, just as with Rachel Inez Lane's "chromosomes that bite like snakes" in her poem "Raised by Wolves," or the millions of cells that "spin away into the invisible" in Madelyn Garner's "The Body's First Lessons," as every day "we are unbodied" yet drop "luminous seeds" to a devouring ground.

It is within the fiction finalist group that the concept of time is explored most palpably: Kellie Wells's "In the Hatred of a Minute," as our fiction editor observes, "reaches into the past to create a modern fable," of what at first seem to be merely personified abstractions ("Time," "History," "God"). Yet this second-prize-winning writer manages to create a layered present of often hilarious characters who, ironically, are dealing with grief and loss, as well as the heckles from the cafeteria at John Dewey Junior High.

First-prize-winning author Sultana Banulescu's "Beggars and Thieves" is a stylistic whirlwind that melds history (Revolution and revolution), and the immediate catastrophic earthquake in Bucharest with Byzantium and Transylvania, and still alludes to a future that will be saved by imagination and the very books that tumble from the sky creating an aftershock, not only of March 24, 1977, but of the mysterious numbers 55-22-64 and the poetry that feeds the soul.

Caitlin Kindervatter-Clark's "The Pygmy Queen" evokes the inner lives of three generations, confined under one Florida roof, trying to distinguish the grandmother's timeless preoccupation with the past and the desperate dream of saving her granddaughter from the wasting pain of the future—even as the birds of prey circle overhead. In contrast, Stephen Taylor's "Jolly Old England," with its bow to the pubs and pints of a father's youth, is a bedtime story created with love by a son just beginning to face the extent of his aging father's confusion.

Appropriately, we end this issue in the secret gardens that are always timeless, with their promise of recurrence and renewal.

Leslie Ringold, photograph

Sideways Glances in the Rear-View Mirror

1.

That's how I watched my first love disappear.
The day I figured *go* and *don't look back,*
I pressed the pedal down, pulled north and hard
onto a straightaway, but I couldn't *not*
look back. I watched the steady progress
of his diminishment in quick eye-flicks,
each short, snatched look an image
in a flipbook I'd fan into a film, replay
for years to come: the epic Could Have Been.
How he, so movie cowboy, did not turn away,
but leaned against his heart-red pickup truck,
took in my disappearance until distance
waved its wand of dust, haze, curvature
of earth. And we were gone. Like that.

2.

Like that. We come and go. Yes. No. Like that.
The way I drove the dark road home at night,
struck something. The right back tire's bump
a certainty, but it was late and icy
so I did not stop. Not true, not true.
Yes, to darkness, ice, to homeward bound,
to secondary road and yes, I did not stop
but no to *something* unless that indistinction
means alive, means animal, means flash
of striped fur, corner of the eye, no stopping
no, there was no time to stop. Groundhog,
I reassured myself—rabid, feral—but the gut
said, well-loved cat. I drove. The mirror served up
darkness, far-off headlights wheeling in black ice.

3.

Against black ice, the Pennsylvania D.O.T.
sprays long white stripes of salt solution
down the asphalt, revamps highway lanes
to guitar fret boards where we play
our private theme songs, variations
of *Keep Moving, No Regrets, Drive On.*
Black ice isn't black, but a slick transparence
taking on the shape and color of what's
underneath. A subtle gloss across the facts
that wipes out variations, incongruities,
turns roads to treacheries, makes memory safe.
The roads we solve with salt. Or time. Or both.
The past requires several mirrors angled
backward: what's gaining on us comes up fast.

4.

What's gaining on us comes up fast: the past
unfixed from time or place. Unlike these highway
signs for measured mile, *begin* and *end*, insisting
that I inventory what's between. I count
winter, January, turnpike unzipping snowfields,
shopping opportunities due west, my adolescent
daughter and her best friend hunkered
in the backseat, deconstructing lyrics
to a love song: Does he really love her?
Did she cheat? Riprap in the gullies, hard
blue sky before the next storm, rivets
every fourteen feet of guardrail, but no
charms, no talismans, no certainties except
the singer's voice unpacking baskets of regret.

5.

The singer's voice unpacks a basket of regret,
bad luck, extenuating circumstances, alibi,
lament, boo-hoo, poor me, lub-dub of tires crossing
bridge joints, but the underlying beating heart's

our own. Last week, a friend remarked *it's funny
how the past keeps changing* and we laughed —
so cleverly we've brushed a shine across our
crimes, our gutlessness, made tragic romance
from the swirling air of swift departures.
How else to live? Except to cook the past,
then sauce it, banquet on it, sure it's richly past,
but still keep glancing in the mirrors lest those fictions
catch up, overtake us as we watch, eyes forward,
for the jackknifed truck, the next catastrophe.

6.

The next catastrophe has packed its suitcase,
separated socks from folded underwear,
is just now leaving the garage. The next
catastrophe is eating escargots, just shot
a cop, is fast asleep, needs OxyContin,
needs it, *now*. The next catastrophe
befell a marketplace last week and soon
you'll see wide angles of its rubble, close-ups
of its bloody infant shoe. What's next is
still developing, still moving toward you
from a backward shack town in the deep past
of your replicating cells, what's next is colorless
and odorless, does not believe in signs,
will take its place, if it takes place, in time.

7.

What's next will take its place in time. Like that.
Yes. No. I hit the brakes, pull into a rest stop.
The past precisely occupies its spot in time.
Fixed there. With rivets. It's not sneaking up on me.
What happens *now* can't make what happened *then*
worse, better. In the backseat, the girls reject this,
roll their eyes, pretend to stick their fingers
down their throats. They argue the romantic view:
how sad the singer feels is proof how much
he loved. Oh no, I say, you're being suckered

by regret sung rough-edged, baritone; you're being
taken by the past. I tell them: everybody's
sorry when the deal is done. You're *old*,
they say, as though that ended it. It does. It will.

8.

It does, it will. The end's the object in
the mirror closer than appears, the end's
the thing that's sneaking up on me. The rest
is gone. Like that. Dust, curvature of earth.
No matter what I wish for, how I sauce it,
twist it, gloss it, name it, dress it into what
it's not but closely seems, what's past is done
and every spun-out version of what *could*
have been like spider silk in time-lapse, all gone
too. No matter how sideways my glances
in which mirror of that shiny trick, the mind,
I look. I pull back onto the straightaway.
The girls replay the song. We sing. I drive.
That's how I watched my first love disappear.

Beggars and Thieves

I

It was March 4th, 1977. My father was in the living room,
reading in his armchair at his desk between the two walled-in
bookcases. My mother was in my bedroom, sitting on the edge
of my bed. She made me read the clock on the nightstand, as she
did every night to make sure I could. It said 9:20 p.m. The door
between the two rooms was open, and all the lamps were lit.

"I can hear it coming," I remember my mother saying. "I can
hear it coming."

"You can't hear it coming," my father called out. "You don't
have them in Transylvania."

"Now I know," she said, turning to me. "It's the rattle."

"Please," my father said. "I was here in Bucharest when the
Carlton Hotel collapsed. You weren't even born."

"I wish I never were," she said, and I wondered what that
actually meant.

"If you don't mind," my father said. "I'm trying to finish *Mrs.
McWilliams and the Lightning*. Does 'Mark Twain' actually mean
anything in the English language?"

"Yes, it does," she said. "Please come stay with us. It's getting closer and closer."

"*The fear of lightning,*" the voice read from the other room, "*is
mostly confined to women.*"

"Will you come stay with us?" she pleaded.

"*Mortimer! Mortimer!*" my father read aloud. "*You know there is
no place as dangerous as a bed in such a thunderstorm as this, all the books
say that; yet there you would lie, and deliberately throw away your life —*"

"Then I will come to you," my mother said. She rose, took
me in her arms because I was unwilling to walk where I didn't
have to, and meant to cross the threshold. We were thrown from
wall to wall and landed in a chair at the other end of the room. I
could hear her head hit the bricks.

"Please do," my father said, without noticing our failed attempt. "Please do. And when you do—"

He didn't finish. I could see him in the mirror on top of my dresser dropping Mark Twain and staring at us in amazement and disbelief through the open doors.

"The Carlton," he stammered. "The Carlton Hotel."

"Dad?" I called out.

"Stay where you are," he shouted. "Don't you move, do you hear me?!"

"Stop shaking," I demanded, and grabbed my mother's arm to steady her.

"I'm not shaking, sweetheart," my mother said. "*The earth* is shaking."

We were hitting the wall, again and again, with that dull sound. The chair was rocking, although it wasn't a rocking chair; it kept getting stuck and unstuck to the wall like a fridge magnet.

"Does it hurt?" I asked.

"A little," and I could hear the pain in her smile. "Sit still."

"I will come to you," my father shouted, struggling to rise from his high, padded armchair.

"Stay where you are," she said gently. "It's not worth it. She won't even remember me."

"Yes, she will," my father said.

"Will you die?" I asked, hearing her skull crack again as we danced that weird dance.

"No," she said. "I will never die. I will always be with you."

The lights went out, and the last I saw in the mirror was the bookcases toppling together over the desk and the armchair in a thundering noise. I was looking at a mountain of books.

"Say your prayers," my mother whispered.

"Why?" I asked, as if I didn't know the answer I dreaded, as if this were her doing not Dad's.

She didn't answer any more.

"Our Father Who art in heaven, hallowed be Thy name, Thy Kingdom come, Thy will be done, on earth—"

The earth stopped shaking.

All was silent and dark, and I remember the birds chirping on the windowsill as if it were early morning. It felt warm outside, too warm for March. Between the two bodies lying in their corners, one clasping me so tight I couldn't get to the other, I was the loneliest five-year-old ever.

"Dad?" I called out when the clock struck 9:30, as I did whenever I couldn't fall asleep.

He was leaning over me.

"How do you feel?" he asked.

"Dizzy," my mother answered, and I marveled as much as anyone now at hearing her speak.

"Fifty-six seconds," he said. "I'm sorry. It usually happens once a century in Bucharest."

"Well, this is your lucky century, then," she shot back. "At least now we can rest easily."

"No, we can't," he said. "We have to get out of here. An aftershock may follow."

"What's an aftershock?" she asked.

"Another earthquake," my father answered. "The rate of aftershocks is inversely proportional to the time elapsed since the main shock. Thus whatever the odds of an aftershock are within the first hour, the second hour will have half the odds of the first and the eighth hour will—"

"Let's get out already," she said. "It's the thirteenth hour in my book. Don't forget yours."

We somehow managed to dig up Mark Twain, who was supposedly a barrel of fun, and headed for what had once been the door, blown away along with the living-room Persian carpet and all my toys on it. My father peered through the darkness as if to check if all the steps were still there.

"I am Dorothy," I said. "My house just flew away to meet the wizard."

"Damn your literature," the Communist Party Secretary who lived above us on the third floor greeted me directly, as he rushed down the spiral staircase like a tornado.

"Careful," my father said. "You might end up in one of her titles."

"I am Dorothy," I repeated.

"Yes, you are," my father said warmly. "All you have to do is trust the powers you have."

As we descended, my father carried me on his shoulders while my mother led the way with a lit candle.

"Watch your step," she said.

"Luna," my father cautioned, "blow that thing out. I smell a gas leak. Moon rays and your shining beauty do the trick for me. By the way, there will be no electricity or running water today."

We reached the ground floor, where we were reunited with the magic carpet.

"Here, Philip," my mother pointed to it at the bottom of the stairs. "I'll carry Cardea, you wrap up her toys. Forget the dolls. This month's craze is the stuffed rabbit and the rubber dog."

"Here's Toto," I said. "I am Dorothy. My house fell on the wicked witch and shut her up."

"Put her down," my father said. "She barely ever walks."

"I don't want her walking tonight," my mother said. "Not on this earth."

Once we were outside, the Embassy of Israel across the street opened the gates of its park to receive the flood of hard-hits. We lived in Bucharest's old Jewish neighborhood, where the owners who survived the war had their houses confiscated by the Communist regime and were displaced by non-Jewish state tenants. The landlord we never met had hanged himself in the basement with a bell cord, and rumor had it that before fastening the knot he had cursed all of us to die before our time.

We joined the noisy infants wrapped in blankets and their mothers clutching boxes of jewelry while my own mother started nursing with bruised hands a deep cut on my father's forehead.

"Tolstoy?" she asked.

"No," he said. "I think it was Balzac. The one that knocked me unconscious, anyway."

"God's last reader left on earth," she said.

"I'd rather die of prose than of poetry," he said.

"But you can't possibly die of poetry," she said, "poetry is light."

"Tell me a story," I asked.

"Make one up for yourself," my father advised.

The young Israeli sentry lit a cigarette. I could see his hands shaking in the moonlight.

"Story! That's all they care about!" cried the old, cantankerous caretaker lady who lived in the basement and who didn't have to pay any rent or utilities. "*She* reads all day long, *he* reads day and night! At least she stops to sleep! And that poor child of theirs, they won't let her go to kindergarten so she won't have to learn all those songs and poems, they said! What is she supposed to do all by herself on the second floor, poor little thing, if nobody pays attention to her? *She starts reading too!* Last week she was calling herself Alice, going down some rabbit hole!"

"She changed her mind," the Party Secretary said. "Now she's Dorothy, waiting for some wizard to take her to the Land of Oz, wherever the hell that might be."

"The Land of Oz," my father said, "is actually very close and can be seen from here, except Comrade Secretary is standing in the light. Would Comrade Secretary have the heart, brain and courage to step towards those bushes? This park is big enough for everyone."

"And it gets worse!" the basement lady cried, ignoring my father. "She's obsessed with titles! She titles things, she titles people, she titles happenings! Last month she wrote a story about a colonel and called it *Too Much Glory*! *Too Much Glory*, mind you, at her age!"

"Do you know what a colonel is?" the first-floor neighbor asked me.

"A colonel," I answered, "is just below a general."

"Why not write about a general, then?" he asked again with that pointed look of his.

"Please," my father said. "Please, Comrade General. *At her age?*"

"I have a story," the General told me. "The Colonnade Complex collapsed tonight. Twelve floors, not one survivor. Your godparents used to live on the top floor, I think—Alba and Remus?"

"Well done, General," my father cut in before I could reply. "A brilliant victory. Come on, darling," he rose from his bench and called out to my mother, "we'll be late for the aftershock."

"Do you remember that terrible storm last fall, the night I lost my kitten and rescued a stray puppy from the flood?" the old scrubwoman screeched in our wake. "Do you know what she did, that heartless little thing? She went ahead and titled the night *Raining Cats and Dogs*!"

She stopped, fingering in terror a moving shadow on the wall of our building. "*It is the ghost of the hanged Jew,*" she cried, "*the rope round his neck, back from the dead to collect rent from his tenants!*"

By then we had reached the first floor of the tower stairwell, and my father lifted me so I could see. The earthquake had made a giant crack in the tower staircase, and an electric cable was swinging loose, dangling in the warm night's breeze.

"*It's the rope,*" the doorwoman cried, "*It's the bell cord! It's the rope!*" and she was carried away into her underground dwellings by the General and the Secretary as her screams grew fainter.

9

"What's your title?" my father asked.

"Hanging Out Together," I said.

The phone rang before he could weigh upon that, but I thought it was quite good.

"Look who's working too," my father said, dug the device from the rubble and picked up.

"This is your local Party Committee," I heard a cavernous voice at the other end of the line. "Is this the home of writer Philip Ezra Canton, author of *The Millionaire's Book*? A survivor was rescued from the top floor of the Colonnade Apartments. Comrade Canton, report to the Emergency Hospital for identification purposes," the voice hung up with a metallic click.

My parents looked at each other.

"Remus," my father said.

"Alba," my mother said.

"He's the great writer," my father said.

"You should be ashamed of yourself," my mother said.

"Why?" I asked; neither cared to answer. As for me, for once I didn't know what I wanted.

"Maybe it's neither," she said after the longest time, to show she never stayed angry for long.

"They wouldn't have called. Luna, as they say, the Party knows best. Give me a suitcase."

"What for?'

"I'll stop by the Colonnade on my way home from the hospital," he answered. "I'll pick up whatever stuff of theirs I see lying around."

She gave him a plastic bag.

"This should hold it all," she said. "Take Cardea with you. Just in case there's an aftershock."

II

At the hospital, my godfather was lying in bed, his eyes wide open, staring at the ceiling.

"Remus," my father said. "How are you feeling?"

My godfather smiled and answered:

"55-22-64."

"It won't happen again," my father said. "Not in our lifetime."

My godfather stared blankly and replied:

"55-22-64."

"Remus," my father shook him gently. "What happened to Alba?"

My godfather paused, seemed to count the ceiling spots, then answered in a different voice: "55-22-64."

"Remus," my father urged. *Do you hear me?*

The door opened and a doctor in a white coat entered the ward.

"What are you shouting for, comrade? You're disturbing all my patients. Oh, I see, this must be your friend, the famous essayist, the one who can do it in one page."

"Will he write again?" my father inquired.

"Well," the doctor said. "His left hand's crushed, but he's right-handed, isn't he?"

"For God's sake," my father burst out. "*Will he write?*"

"Comrade, again, there's no need to shout. Yes, he will write."

"When?" my father asked.

"Sometime. He almost flew off from his twelfth-floor balcony," the doctor said, and left.

We stayed so long I still remember the spot pattern on that wet-stained, dripping ceiling.

✿ ✿ ✿

By the time we filled two bottles of rusty tap water behind the nurses' backs, queued for milk, settled for juice and reached the Colonnade, it was late morning. Hordes of newly homeless people were squatting beside the ruins, with burning eyes and parched lips. It was unseasonably warm.

"I'm thirsty," I said.

"Drink slowly," my father said. "And leave your mother some water for her coffee."

"Comrade," a man dangled an empty plastic cup in front of us. "A drink of water. I'll pay."

"I'm not done yet," I protested.

"You've got all that juice," my father spoke sharply.

The man drank the water uncontrollably, wiping his forehead with the precious copper-red drops escaping the corners of his mouth, as if he were bleeding to death.

"Thank you, sir," he said, jingling the cup he had now poured some change into. "There's not one drop of mineral water left in the city, and we've got to save the milk for the children."

My father shook his head and gave the second bottle we had stolen to those closest to him.

"I am looking for a woman," he said. "Her name is Alba."

"Alba?" an old Gypsy woman said. "Alba the poet? The one who lived in the block of flats across the street, where the Party moved all those writers, painters, and musicians, so it could keep an eye on all of them at once? Luckily there's more artists in the capital of the Socialist Republic of Romania than these twelve floors could hold, otherwise now there wouldn't be a single one left."

"What happened to Alba?" my father asked doggedly.

"Well," the Gypsy neighbor said. "You know all these artists were brought here only a few months ago, so none of them had home phone lines installed yet. Alba and her husband were expecting a guest for dinner last night, you know, that other poet who lives in the Jewish neighborhood, he was supposed to bring them an article to publish. He didn't come on time, and since the stores had closed Alba gave me this big bill and asked me for some change so she'd be able to call him. Remus looked the number up and called it out from their window on the top floor, 55-22-64, and you know Alba, her head full of verse, she looked not left or right as she crossed the street to the phone booth, and got run over by a taxi. Her leg's broken, and the driver took her straight to the Emergency Hospital, *except all that Remus saw from the top floor were the marble columns on the other side crushing the phone booth when he stepped out on the balcony moments before the earthquake.*"

My father sat on the edge of the ruins of the Colonnade Row Apartment Complex and buried his face in his hands, overcome with a mix of emotions.

"I forgot," he whispered. "I lost track of time. I was reading."

I pulled his sleeve and forced him to look up.

"What's your title?" I asked.

"You tell me," he said angrily. "You tell me, Cardea, what your title is. Because I have none. Now stay put while I dig for some of their belongings. They'll need whatever I can find."

"You won't find anything," a few Gypsies said wearily. "Right after the earthquake, after we rescued what little we had, thieves came in the middle of the night and robbed us of everything. It came easier than any other night, we had no doors left to lock and were fumbling in the dark, while they had knives and flashlights. Just before leaving, they saw Remus' left mangled hand sticking out from the ruins and they bent to pull the wedding ring from his finger. *'I am alive,'* Remus spoke in the night. *'I am a writer. Who are you?' 'We are thieves,'* they answered outright, *'and we came to plunder.' 'Can you get me out of here?'* Remus asked. *'We will try,'* the head of the thieves answered, and they toiled for two hours to free him from the ruins, and when they got him out he fainted."

"Here," my father said, as he handed me a flower vase. "You hold this. The rest is gone."

"There's this book still, right here," other people said. "Maybe it was theirs. It has no covers, though, so we'll never know."

"Tell me a few lines," my father said. "Maybe I'll be able to guess what it is."

"You must have read a lot," they laughed.

The man who had drunk the water took the battered pages in his hands.

"Dedication," he read. *"In Byzantium all things were two-sided, like a coin. The imperial scholar Procopius of Caesarea wrote two Histories: an official one, in which he praises Justinian and Theodora, and a second, secret one, where he blames the emperor and the empress for all evil on earth. Byzantium was pomp, gold, diamonds, confusion, the art of living as in a dream, a two-faced, big-hearted world; and I dedicate this book of verse to you, for they call you The Millionaire, not for the wealth and fortune you do not have, you never had and you will never have, but for the richness of mind which you so easily squander for the sake of others."*

"Oh," my father said. "This one Remus and Alba can get any time. Keep it for yourself."

"Are you sure?" the man asked.

"I'm sure," my father answered.

I always resented the way he gave his books to strangers for free, but I could never help it.

"Byzantium," another man said. "When was that?"

"Long before we moved here," a woman answered.

"Maybe that's what it all is, a dream," a third man said. "Maybe we'll all wake up tomorrow and find out we never lived at the Colonnade."

The man who had drunk the water jumped on top of the ruins. He still held the coverless book in his hand. His blue eyes were dancing and gleaming with joy.

"All those writers, and painters, and musicians," he said. "I'm sorry for them. I don't have much schooling. But I am alive," and he extended his arm in a joyful salute.

"Toss it," my father advised, since the book seemed to get in the way of something better.

"Are you sure?" the man asked again.

"Unlike history or archeology," my father shrugged, "poetry is light. Toss it like a coin."

By now it was high noon. The book flew like a bird, and landed at the feet of the Party Secretary, who had appeared, dressed in a fireman's uniform, directing a television crew that filmed the ruins.

"Over here," he said. "Over there. And over there."

When the loose pages hit the ground he turned and saw me, still clutching the flower vase.

"You again?!" he said – "damn your literature!"

"I warned you," my father told him, "but you wouldn't listen. It's the third time you cross her. Now you'll end up in one of her titles."

"Too bad we didn't move you all here on time," the Secretary said.

"Too late," my father said. "After tonight, it's too late for patriotic songs and poems."

"At this age, she'll forget," the Secretary said.

"No, she won't," my father said.

"By the way," the Secretary said. *"I forgot.* The Jew had a wife. She got a couple of hours to pack, so I'm afraid she had to leave her furniture behind. As a collector, I'd say she had good taste."

"I've had it," my father said. He turned towards me. "Give me a title for all this. Now."

"Careful," the Secretary said, leaning towards me. "Careful. *Watch your step—*" and I could see him leaning over the banister of the spiral staircase, grinning like a wolf.

"Cardea, you have a way with words," my father told me. "People who know me say you got it from me. That's not true. It's your own way, not mine. Help me out here. Show 'em."

"Show me," the Secretary laughed.

"I am waiting," my father said.

"So am I," the Secretary said.

"I will always be with you," my father said.

"There's nowhere to go," the Secretary said.

Caught between the two of them, under the people's giant stare, I suddenly lost my balance on the edge of the ruins and I almost dropped Remus and Alba's last remaining keepsake. I looked down and I saw I had tripped on a broken discarded flashlight where they'd dug up Remus.

"*Beggars and Thieves*," I blurted out.

"There you go," my father said.

Kathryn Dunlevie, *Carceri del Vaticano*,
mixed media on panel, 60" x 47"

The Grace of Memory

One day, sooner than I wish to think,
the solidity of you
—the deep anchor of your bass voice
that first stunned and then gently
drew me to you so long ago,
and yes—your bewitching beard,
your ardor and signature touch
will go forever missing.
How will I begin to bear it
—how will I endure? Once

you had me close my eyes
and asked me to say when
I might feel the brush of
a clump of eiderdown
laid in the palm of my hand.
I stood there dumbly waiting
and felt nothing at all.
But when I opened my eyes,
there it was—its light presence
so palpably there—
right in the palm of my hand.

Italian Made Simple

tells the story of Mario and Marina,
     and by the end of Chapter 1, I've got it:
the *r* is a *ð*, and Mario and Marina
     will fall in love, he an American
planning a business trip to Italy,
     she an Italian teaching English
in a school *in centro*, downtown,
     which I take to mean Wall Street,
maybe Tribeca or Nolita.
     For the first lesson, they meet
in Marina's *ufficio*, where they repeat
     the half-dozen Italian phrases for *hello*.
Both of them remain patient,
     cheerful, even, in the face of their task.
They name every single blessed thing
     on the desk. What good fortune it is
they cannot yet say, so many small things
     here before them: the pen, the paper, and
the pencil, too, the newspaper, the lamp.
     Marina pronounces each word slowly
while Mario watches her lips, repeats.
     What is this? Marina asks in Italian.
What is this? and Mario, under a spell,
     answers, although he cannot yet
be said to understand these words
     that are little more to him than sounds,
air blown through the shapes
     that Marina's lips make his lips make.
By Chapter 4, simple Italian leads Mario
     and Marina to the window, to the words
for *street, hospital, bicycle, child,*
     where simplicity threatens to abandon
these two people who are just trying

to live, an idiomatic expression
for *to make money. No,* says Marina.
  That is not a child. That is not a girl.
a woman, a car, etcetera. Mario loves
  the word *eccetera,* which he figures
will save him lots of time. When their time
  is up, Mario and Marina walk to the door,
at exactly the same moment say *la porta.*
  The next moment, they laugh. *Eccetera,*
eccetera. Because I cannot live
  in the simple present, where *Italian Made*
Simple begins, I read ahead.
  In Florence, on his business trip,
Mario buys for Marina a gold bracelet.
  A gold bracelet Mario buys for Marina.
Mario for Marina buys a gold bracelet.
  He does not yet understand that Marina
already knows that he loves her,
  that she has loved him since Chapter 5,
Familia, wherein Mario showed quick
  concern for her ill niece. Mario, alone
in Florence, on the far side of his voyage
  through the definite pronouns, the prepositions,
the baffling procession of possessive forms,
  Mario sits at a café, drinking
the beverage he ordered by mistake.
  When the waitress sets it brightly before him,
Piacere, Mario says, ever gracious.
  Mario, at the end of my textbook,
of your slow, sometimes laborious story,
  how will I live without you?
You do not yet know that the final lesson
  finds you and Marina deciding to marry,
to live in Rome, yet here, in Chapter 20,
  Firenze, still you sip and savor.
You open your dictionary.
  The small table at which you sit
is called *tavolino,* just as you had thought,
  and you smile to yourself,
now that you are lonely, now that you know
  you know by heart,
the meaning of every single blessed thing.

Amazing

Amazing the number of people who, on learning
        that you live on Elm Street, make a joke about the movie.
                Amazing, too, the delight they find in their own wit

so contagious that you, almost always, have to laugh along with them,
        this circumstance surely a piece of Heaven fallen to earth,
                although little do these people know that the nightmare,

the real nightmare, happened on Pine Street, the corner of Pine Street
        and Elm, one day six years ago, when Patty, home early
                from her shift at the hospital, pulled up

in front of her house, 5 Pine, and decided
        to walk to the Elm Street Deli, for a pack of cigarettes.
                Behind the counter, Andre was watching the TV

tuned to his favorite investment program, today's
        best opportunity blaring past the pegboard display
                of aspirin and eyeglass repair kits. Andre nodded to the TV

as he handed Patty her change, saying, *I'm retiring early, Pat*,
        and Patty shot back, *Yeah, me too. I'm beat*.
                So far so good. Until Patty, halfway across the street,

ready to light up, saw her car: roof crushed,
        windshield cracked into approximately
                a million pieces held together by some law of physics

11th graders know for two weeks. And so Patty ran back
        for Andre, the two of them ending up at the front fender,
                speechless. Andre noticed the pine-scented cardboard tree

still dangling from the rear-view mirror. Andre noticed details.
        You can't own a deli a block from a high school
                and not notice details: soda can up the sleeve, bagel

down the pants, beef jerky down the pants.
        Andre noticed, at the car's front left wheel,
                a rock the size of a softball, but reddish and rough.

It was as hot as toast from Hell. Andre, always quick, ready
    for any opportunity, had touched the rock,
        briefly. *Yikes,* he said, *Holy shit! Do you know what this*

is, Pat? A meteor. Then, because anyone would have to
    say the words in order to process it, Andre announced,
        in his best imitation of the cable-TV investment advisor,

Pat, your car's been hit by a meteor. And it was true,
    confirmed by the police and the high school science teacher.
        Down the block a nightmare, if you want to think of it

that way, likewise the newspaper reporters and photographers
    another nightmare, of sorts: papers to sign,
        questions to answer as kids from the high school

pushed at each other and watched. Patty crumbled her cigarette
    in the pocket of the green hospital scrubs
        in which that morning she'd delivered

the unexpected news that a CAT scan was still clean,
    in which she'd pried open the fist of a man's
        irrefutable conviction that this should not be happening,

there should not be tubes running into his arms,
    other tubes running out from under his blanket.
        It's a nightmare, earth, where Heaven is when

near-disaster outraces disaster. Equally nightmare, if you want
    to think of it that way: that we can live in the face of this,
        as does the elderly couple Patty saw that morning

in the hospital gift shop,
    the woman no longer able to name the pink roses
        the man placed in her arms, folded her arms to hold.

As Patty spelled her name for a reporter, it struck her
    that everyone gathered on the corner of Elm and Pine
        was with her in a horror movie so bad it is good,

and a light that maybe was a camera-flash, and maybe not,
    made even the tall pierced kid
        who spat, and tapped a cigarette on his palm,

bobbing his head to some private tune, made even him
    look like a piece of Heaven fallen to this earth
        where Patty, as if out of the blue, saw

that had she quit smoking, as she'd been trying, for 53 days,
    she might have sat five minutes longer in her car,
        listening to the oldies station, craving nothing

but the part where Stevie Wonder sings, *that's why*
    I'll always be around, yeah, yeah, yeah, yeah,
        and Patty nodded and shivered and had to laugh

as she saw herself at the steering wheel, singing, as the meteor
    wheeled above Elm Street, no, Pine Street,
        yes, Pine.

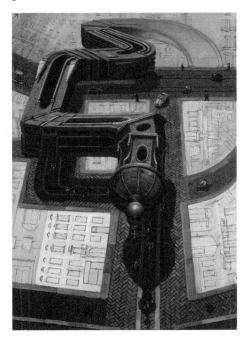

Alexander Shundi, *Following the Shadow*, oil on canvas, 42" x 29"

Nocturne from the North Carolina Aquarium at Pine Knoll Shores

At dusk, after the Yellow
Perch have clustered in
their classes—each fish sculpting its sea
horse of green bottle glass.
After men have unpinned the "Fat-
lips Minnow and Gray Triggerfish"
name badges from their chests,

we sit and listen as the river
slows, the water deepens. As I
wonder what I should be called after
this—with the mop-head
wrung, the vacuum tube
coiled—watching the snow-
capped tortoise shells sink like glaciers,

feeling as though I could live
inside the bell of the Moon
Jellyfish, beneath the twisted cone
of the Hermit Crab. Because they too
are alone, with the hours left to be
swept. We rub out the faces of children,
where their noses and cheeks have smudged

the glass. On the exhibit plaque
for the Largemouth Bass, I read,
"it is known to take any bait
it considers alive. Some have
been found, they say, their mouths
punctured, from being caught
and let go, let go so many times."

Drinking the Gin of Time

1
The cartographer rented the attic room
in the first version. He mapped houses of wood,
and waves of trees, filled in the spaces
that evenings made, indigo-blue and oriole-
orange, weighted the outlines black, colored
the peninsulas green. Drinking the gin
of time, he grew transparent as air.
At his sheerest, he laid down divides,
manicured the Caribbean and smoothed
the Aegean's edges. Uncle-lodger

or cousin enigma—it was he we
were kind to in the first draft. He kept
each place in its border, neatly arranged,
each island aloof, wrapped in its blue binding,
like little boats sleek in the offing.

2
Afternoons on Meridian, I practiced
piano, hands too large to mind rules.
Or my mother cut my black-red hair
in a pageboy, evened the ends with a bowl.
We played too at being kind to Father who
mapped the times between this day and that
by driving away to work. He could not stay put.
The blue sky poured in hourglass shapes between
the juniper trees, then waited. The time
was told from sky and earth and light on the roof-tiles'
overlapping smiles. It filled the whiles
between this and that, between what I'd do
and when—like sky weathering its waiting,
the dust motes lit like stars, time's visible wheat.

3
You caught the feel of me, Father, awkward
in blue and white oxfords,
photoed feet-first, boat-footed,
splay-legged, soles enlarged.
So, I had come into the world.

Lucky the shoes weighted me down,
grounded me when earth-
quakes rolled through:
once I rode the ground swell
face-down on grass, stubble
itching to meet me.
Earth's waves and furrows
were like ocean's, all crescendo.

Everything, even the feathers of grass
on sea-cliffs, was ruffled,
but I stood again, anvil-footed,
grounded, not thrown off
flailing into space.

4
Father, I do not think your ashes speak.
Pearl-white, slate-gray,
mourning-dove blue, you are
your suit of ashes now.

The birds won't tell—
awl-beaked cowbird,
red-winged blackbird,
tools to open what you
guarded like a word.

In boxes dense and sleek
as polished teak,
you hoarded speech
as other fathers hoarded coins.

Now you're milk of ash the rain
can wash your silence in.

5
But the girl who once was me
is no less opaque, her air of doing
shown in the solemn mouth, puckered as she draws
cats, clouds, doorways, stairs. She colors in
the witness-dogs and birds, the postman,
the gardener—eager-eared, he's bent toward
the irises' ear trombones. My father
is wearing his felt hat and gabardine
raincoat, cloaked in the fatherly mystery

of work. He's off again this morning. I'm home,
drinking the milk of sleep at lunch. Later, my eyes
itch with sleep like inklings of the mystery.
It bathes me even in dreams persistently
and without mercy, leaving these grains
like seeds in the corners of my eyes.

6
Meridian's golden this morning
with bourbon of autumn light. Phases of apples
rise and set in the apple trees. Here's one—
red-skinned, gold-marled, bird-pecked. The eaten
half, a moon-colored cheek, part sunken, browns
on the ridges and peaks the birds have left.
Fermenting on lawns, the wind apples sun
in time, drown in ripening weather.

Will they be cider or vinegar? The apples'
rosewood tears, the seeds, don't know. As if mourning
weren't already implied. The afternoon's crisp,
its cloud-edges chilled and lit. Tomorrow, the air
will be quilled with ice bits. Time and the weather
breed trees from tears when the light's just right.

7

Driving his truck of windows down Meridian,
the glassman arrives. The flotsam and jetsam
of door jambs, window sills framing the dusty
weather of couches, a lattice-work birdcage
on a porch, a red door, float by. He carries
the windowed world. He is wearing
the stars of Texas on his blue leather boots,
a sombrero wide as his shoulders. He's
puma-colored like the grasses of hillsides
in summer. He carries the smell of hillsides
and weather, and gingerly, the sheets of eye-food
inside. Will he stop by your house, or drive on,
delivering the weather, the transparency?

8

Meridian Avenue's abstaining this
morning from morning. Unfinished houses—
diagram doorways, stick-figure halls—let in
the blue. The wood's peach-blush red, resinous,
its pine fumes bathing the street like sun.
Three staircases climb the cloudlessness
between thunderheads, past the blond light
I'm seeing near the cottonwoods. No one's
shuffled yet through poplar leaf-heaps; hand-wide,
yellow arrows, they feint and point in all directions.

They baffle the crows. Three skinny waterfalls
go nowhere on the rock faces Meridian
faces across the Missouri. As if time weren't
already rushing in the falling water,
as if the hush of distance
were really suspension.

9

The water lightened my mother's head
then poured off her body as she stepped
up the swimming pool's turquoise tiled stairs.
Curve-cornered, they shimmered while the lap
and net of light on water tugged as she rose

and spun her its cellophane glove, its robe
of glowing. Still, she could not quite
walk out of her skin, her feet weighted
with gravity's thick soles. Now I too am
fifty, and can't walk out of my skin, the scam
of wrinkles and pouts. These warm nights, I float
on the pool's traffic of weather and stars.
It lies above and beside me, its stillness
a ruse I am in, like water for skin.

10
Today, the air's pewter with humidity's haze.
Silver maple leaves seethe in the trees.
The world's our laundromat, our sauna.
Sun-tea brews in a jar, nervous reservoir
of light, vibrating on the sun-drenched
porch planks as I rock in the shade.
I'm weighted with humidity, warted
with sweat. I'd like to be bodiless,
a scarf, a pointillist print. I'd float
on spaces like thought, a driftwood mobile,
made from scraps of weather and sleep. The porous
bits of tide caught in the oak-bark almost
balance the motes of time held in the pieces of pine.

11
What drives my father along the transparent
meridian of his path on earth? The engine
of time runs silent by day, spinning
views by as he circles the earth: Ohio's
teal-green hills touching the Missouri's
sheer cliff faces; Omaha's undulant
highways nudging the rivers of air
in Marin. Everywhere, memory

is in the air. Sequoias are touching
the Eastern locusts' migrations; the horse-
tail ferns are brushing the moon. Under the stars'
animal outlines, he draws this sheer line
like an indigo rafter arcing above us.
It marks *before* and *after, once* and *ago.*

12

Now the meterman comes, to read
the ergs of work, love, hope, and despair.
He wears a gray fedora and tips it
as he climbs the metal stairs to the attic.

Each step is embossed with stars, time-slurred,
foot-smoothed, but engineered
to prevent slippage. Even travelers
drunk on gin can safely reach haven here.

The reader of meters goes on, his path in time
a series of U's, from sidewalk, to meter,
to sidewalk and back. He greets each meter like
a friend, a text he knows how to read.

Perhaps he can read the watts of love,
the mystery ergs of work, the eager
volts of desire, or record the charges
and urges of words, lodged in the pores

of wood or afloat like spores of rainfern
in humid air: words and their motes, wisps
of the almost-heard. Listen—whispers afloat
in air's transparency, the gin of time.

In the Hatred of a Minute

When Time was a little girl, she couldn't wait to grow up. At four, no stranger to blood, she got her period. At six she married a train conductor. Nobody ever loved her so well as the train conductor. Except perhaps the country of Switzerland. History, who walked around with warheads and that inaugural wheel and fightin' words and a triceratops or two and the Golden Horde and creation myths featuring a landscape cobbled together from the hips and breasts and randomly strewn extremities of a savaged body and the Big Bang and bombardiers and bad decisions and Stonehenge and a Flat Earth and its dead partisans and the Vin Fiz Flyer and blazing villages and Marie Antoinette and multiple paradigm shifts and the Bronze Age and Aramaic and slave ships and the tell-tale iridium layer blanketing the bones of dinosaurs and the pathological insecurities of despots—all falling from his mouth—had mixed feelings about her. He depended on her but sometimes thought of her as his bitch. Unlike the train conductor, he was impossible to kiss. He liked facts more than theories, men more than women, war more than peace, the victor more than the vanquished, carrots more than parsnips, and had not been a good father to Historicity and Historiography, latchkey offspring who raised themselves from a tender age. History does not like to think of himself as a nightmare from which a famous fictional character cannot awake. Writers are all such gloomy gusses, thinks History, they should just leave him out of it, honestly. History, History feels compelled to point out, never did anything without the will and sanction of nettled men.

But Time, she's always passing, dying 86,400 deaths a day. Time hasn't time enough for fear or grief. Or knitting. Or long walks along the beach. Woodworking. Kickboxing. She once tried tai chi, but it made her anxious. As does the soothing music piped into the waiting rooms of dentists; she could grind her crowns to dust listening to that. Time wears a cardigan so as not to freeze.

Time has always wanted to travel to the moon, in a sleeping berth, rocked to sleep by the rhythmic wobble of the rocket. In the absence of gravity, her bones and purpose would thin and she'd become more mollusk than sundown, more inchworm than equinox. She'll make that possible one day, discount travel to other planets. *In Time are all things possible*, Time's mother used to tell her after she came home from a long, hard day of being heckled by those geniuses she went to John Dewey Junior High with: *Time passes*, they crowed as she walked by, *just like gas!* That had made her persona non grata in the cafeteria. Time's mother told her to just take it a day at a time, things were bound to improve, junior high would not last forever. Time shuddered at the thought.

Though she received the usual training, Time does not understand the concept of light-years or the evolution and high octane death of stars, does not understand how she might only be gazing at a memory, at a history, when she looks at the light-spangled sky, at a long dead brightness, seeing the star as it was a thousand years ago. No, she does not understand how it can be true that she's staring at deaths that have not yet caught up with the dying, slow-as-molasses extinctions that have not yet reached the eyes of the beholder, thermonuclear reactions she authorized years ago. Time looks at the sky throbbing with light and makes herself think, *That star is ten light-years away and, though it's now an adult, what I'm witnessing is its childhood*. All those dead children hanging in the sky. Who can bear to exist in the face of that? Time stops thinking. For Time, things happen when they happen. And things are always happening. Time's dance card is always full.

Time's sister, Emily, was recently diagnosed with a fatal illness that will cause her body to fail organ by organ. There will be a cure for this disease in the future, some years after Emily will have died, at the age of sixteen.

Time imagines looking in the sky and seeing eight-year-old Emily chasing the other perishing stars with a butterfly net.

A famous man, friend of History's (they can be so terribly dull, though this one harbored a boyhood tenderness for silver foxes and loved to twinkle on the tips of his hammertoes in an imagined *pas de deux* when alone in his bedchamber), once said that Time was God's way of preventing all things from occurring at once, and this made her feel purposeful, even if she could ill afford to be a groupie of someone who nourishes himself thin as a slip on timelessness. She and God have gone round on this point before, when she has urged him to imagine an ending, a grand finale, a way out, an omega. *Just think about it*, she says slyly (for God, thinking is as good as doing). He doesn't seem happy with the way things are going anyway, always brooding, talk about a gloomy gus. History will continue to bluster about God even after he's gone. He'd become glamorous in death, a source of wistful longing, imagine the teary obituaries, the memorial cook-offs, there would be protests and rallies to resuscitate him, people would plant lilies in formerly sacred places instead of setting themselves and others ablaze, wouldn't that be nice for a change? Time was all about change. There was a time when God was thought to be dead, before his penumbra was sighted hovering over Peoria, Illinois. Time has pointed out to God that she is meat and milk of many religions. Without her there could be no Second Coming, no Ancient of Days, no day of Brahma, no Dreamtime, no eternity, no spinning Kalachakra, and certainly no apocalypse or End Times with which to harrow the brethren. God is careful not to look Time in the face, for if he did he might be fixed in place on the spot, and then where would he be? And when? Time sometimes whispers in his ear as he casts a remorseful gaze across the clearcut forest of the future, old growth felled and gone, *Your Time has come.*

God tries to imagine what would happen to the universe were he no longer its custodian, its bricoleur, its brawny doorman, its stenographer, its documentarian, its midwife, its wetnurse, its internist-alienist-mesmerist-iridologist, its sniper, its puppeteer. Would it be better off? He's made some mistakes. Not intervening in suffering, for example, as though he were just a naturalist tracking a pride of starving lions, one who felt it was his duty to remain at an impartial distance and let nature do what nature does, which is eat things, so when that baby elephant comes along, frantically searching for its herd after a sandstorm, all he can do is close his eyes and keep the camera rolling. Yes, that was one rule he regretted. But he doesn't think it's hubris to believe that without him all motion would screech to a halt, all mass would begin to transmogrify and come to resemble the diaphanous and hesitant radiance that is the Creator, and this might not be such a desirable thing; to be cast in his image is to see a ravenous absence when you walk by a mirror. One theologian-turned-agnostic called God (a little spitefully, he thought, no need to resort to name-calling, nothing more scornful than a convert to disbelief) a pandemic, and God began to see himself this way too and sometimes he wished there were a vaccine, but these are thoughts God indulges only once every billion years—why should he listen to humans, those misanthropic toddlers of the universe?—and then he tucks them away in the deepest, most bottomless recesses of his unconscious (what those nosy string theorists are always trying to lasso), and now he bats Time aside, which causes her to reel, and in that moment, in *that* moment, *this* moment, every sleeping creature dreams of an orphaned mitten and an empty bottle sitting atop a mountain inhabited only by a dying glacier, but then Time settles and she tends to the day, her overgrown garden, weeds the minutes and tills the hours. *Your Time has come and gone,* she whispers to herself. And then the dreamers wake with only a faint residue of the abjection of having been abandoned by Time and they slap walls as they walk and drink glass upon glass of water.

When Time and Emily were children, they played the misfortune and torture game. *Would you rather be born without feet or constantly sneeze glass, a bloody handkerchief always falling from your pocket?* asked Emily. Time had a thing about the hygiene of handkerchiefs, as Emily well knew, so the choice was an easy one. And in fact footlessness, she thought, might be useful in slowing a girl down. She'd been accused of lolloping more than once. *Would you rather kill everyone you've ever known and loved or be the salve the wounded apply to their weeping sores?* asked Time, and Emily looked at her mournfully and laid her tiny hand upon her shoulder.

Time is everyone's favorite assassin.

Time learned to drive and received her learner's permit when she was eight and she careened about recklessly as if there were no tomorrow, a dream she sometimes had. But there was and she woke to see snow covering the family Corvair like a winter pelt. It made Time long for a durable pet, maybe a Giant Tortoise, a loudmouthed macaw, something that could at least see her through to the next century, if not the one after that. That morning she did poorly on her algebra quiz. Sometimes Time failed math on principle.

Time feels abstract, her heart flutters. She cannot see her knees.

By the time Time was 4.5 billion years old, she'd seen some things, things that made even God turn the sound down. She watched as human beings, those Johnny-come-latelies, ate every-thing around them, leaving behind dental impressions on every ex-tinction. Time was born with a stubborn nostalgia and she missed the dodo even before it squawked and stumbled gracelessly in and out of existence.

Once Time went to her in-laws' house for Easter dinner, and she ate only scalloped potatoes and Parker House rolls. The train conductor's mother sniffed accusingly and intimated that Time had been packing it on lately and would be wise to watch her figure, go easy on the starch. She made a joke about the fullness of Time. The train conductor's mother was no will-o'-the-wisp herself, but Time kept her trap shut. She spooned four wizened peas onto her plate. Then the train conductor's mother told Time she had an all-natural cream with aloe and almond oil that might help deflate the bags beneath her eyes. Time had not slept since she was three years old. Preparing eternally for the future can keep a girl from getting the proper shut-eye, but there was no explaining this to the train conductor's mother, who was not a career woman and who slept like a truckload of lead and snored like a jackhammer. "Your eyes look like they're packed and ready for a long trip!" hooted her husband's mother. Time swallowed a pea and told her mother-in-law the date and hour of her death, and her mother-in-law spent the rest of the meal dabbing spittle from the corner of her mouth and plucking cloves from the ham's glazed backside.

Later, Time would feel regretful and make her mother-in-law forget, though she'd retain a persistent and nagging unease in the presence of Time and would always sit with her back to the wall.

Contrary to popular belief, Time, a fretful traveler, never flies, but she does enjoy walking. She believes it impolite to arrive at a destination too quickly. Sometimes even bicycling gives her the bends.

When her husband comes home at night, after an arduous day of conducting, he likes Time to stop and throw her arms about his neck. In this glistering second: _ _ _ nobody dies. Bodies accumulate like corncobs at a picnic. The universe explodes with excessive human occupancy every day at 6 p.m. sharp.

At 6:01, the world suffers anew.

When Time was 38, she burned her hand on a waffle iron, and now her lifeline looks like it's incarcerated, and it makes her miss her father, who made burnt waffles for her and her sister once while on weekend furlough, the only bread they ever broke together. Time heals slowly, so slowly, more slowly than you might imagine.

Truth is, Time and God dated for a short time when Time was in college. She never told the train conductor about this as he already suffers from feelings of inadequacy and he needs to be alert at work, not measuring himself against impossible standards for heaven's sake. This was when Time was a contortionist, mostly on weekends, bendable as a whip of licorice, how she put herself through school. Budding physicists paid good money to watch Time bend, watch her gyrate behind glass. They tried to coax her to talk about how she started, and sometimes she told them a story, both true and not, as all stories are, about a broken home, father in and out of the slammer, a mother who worked double shifts at the cog and fob factory, and a little brother with a mysterious illness who could never go out in the sun, who played alone in moonlight as other children's eyes quivered with dreams. The physicists sobbed as they pretended to dandle Time on their knees and stroke her silken cheeks, tried to think how they could save her from this sordid life born of unfortunate circumstances. And then the curtain fell.

One of the many problems that doomed Time's romance with God was that he was never on time, and no amount of couples counseling (to which he invariably arrived late and full of breath-less excuses—he made it clear he just wasn't comfortable talking about their problems with a stranger; oh, and that was another problem, God's passive-aggression—the Old Testament days of God, then in his adolescence, blowing his stack and drowning the universe at the faintest aggravation, those days were long gone, and though Time was grateful for this, weary as she was of start-ing over and over and over again, still she wished he'd learn to express his anger more directly and to compartmentalize less; that, she thought, had begun with enumerating the deadly sins, among which Time thought there was a *lot* of overlap, whether God saw it or not, gluttony, for example, just another species of lust, *Am I right?* she asked the therapist), no amount of therapy would ever make God punctual (just ask those sadsack Millenarians).

God complained that he could hear Time ticking at night, like a bomb set to detonate upon sunrise, and it kept him more awake than usual, doubly omniscient, when what he really craved was a little ignorance, a little amnesia, so he stopped staying over.

Time, at her most lithe and flexible, *supple as string*, the physicists had said admiringly, used to lie awake at night worrying about the paradox of time travel and autoinfanticide—what if she traveled back in time and killed herself? (Many braggarts had claimed to kill Time, had claimed to waste her—she was forever getting death threats—but here she was still kicking, no bucket in sight, the sun going up, the sun going down. . . .) And then that would mean that she would never have existed, which would mean she never traveled back in time in the first place, indeed there'd be no time in which to travel had Time been aborted in the womb, so, erm. . . . Wait. A. Minute. It was at this moment that all sleeping people dreamed of the maudlin faces of handless clocks and woke up feeling so fatigued they realized it was actually the day before yesterday and took a slug of NyQuil so they could make it through the night to reach tomorrow one more time, eye teeth and pie-in-the-sky aspirations more or less intact.

God tried to explain to Time the Novikov Self-Consistency Principle, but there was such an air of superiority in his tone as he maundered on and on about *many worlds* and *quantum suicide* and the mortality of cats kept in the malevolent boxes of theorists and a man who becomes immortal shooting himself again and again with a loaded gun that refuses to fire la-lala that she set the phone down and scrambled some eggs. She did the dishes, made a grocery list, cleaned out the crumb tray of her toaster, and picked up the phone again in time to hear God say, "Will I see you later?"

In the hospital room, Emily is surrounded by wheezing machinery and the usual life-sustaining drips, and she tells Time that she understands now what it means to be alone, but sometimes she imagines the tubes are tunnels through which a tiny civilization passes in and out of her body on their way to and from their jobs, the opera, the bank, their homes, each twinge of pain a pileup on the highway that leads to a failing interior, a torture she remembers from long ago, and then she understands that it is she who is lying in a room that dwells in the body of another, and she feels suddenly molecular and weightless, as though her skin were turning to starlight, and she is less afraid.

It's not that Time can't cry; it's that she's crying all the time, but nobody sees it. Her sorrow, the sad set of her mouth, the smudge of despair beneath her eyes, are invisible to others, announcing as they do the coming of loss, and loss, and loss, and that's her misfortune, her Cassandra Torture. Time says, "You'll always have me, Em," and Emily touches the place on Time's chin from where the invisible tears drop and says, "That's just what I don't have," and her mouth tries to smile.

On God and Time's first date, they went to a slasher film, God's choice, and God gasped five seconds before every out-of-nowhere chop of the ax. A man sitting in front of them turned around and glowered at God, who smiled apologetically, and then, midway through the movie, the man made a show of springing from his seat, throwing a snarl behind him, and stomping up the aisle. "Non-believer," God whispered to Time.

When Time told God she thought it was better if they were just friends, God called her a cruel mistress. God knows, God was used to rejection, but he'd expected more from Time. He whinnied like a horse and balled his hands into fists, the floor began to tremble, objects hopped off shelves, and then the gathering squall in his eyes passed and he promised to work on his shortcomings (or longcomings, whichever were more irksome, he'd change, he promised), but Time said she didn't want to change him and that she knew there were plenty of people in the world that loved God just the way he was, warts and all. God sighed so windily that Time fell backwards, and all of a sudden there was Abraham Lincoln, whose drawn face looked like molten tallow, and Marie Curie blinking amidst the glow that trailed her, there they were standing in the room between God and Time, looking a little shopworn and dispossessed. History, who hated it when someone speculated what Genghis Khan and Mary Magdalene and Antony van Leeuwenhoek and Tutankhamun and Harriet Tubman would say to each other if they time-traveled and ended up discussing the important questions of the day over dinner, snorted contemptuously. Time picked herself up and marched forward and when she did Abraham and Marie flew bass-ackwards out the window like balloons suddenly unstrangled. She imagined she knew now why the melted features of the president's face sloped to the side like windblown wax.

Shortly after, History, an opportunist, saw his chance and asked Time out. Time said, "It's over between us," and History said, "But we've never been together," and Time said, "See?"

Some weeks later History thought of a clever comeback, so he phoned Time up and said, in a fleering tone, "One person's past . . . is another's future!" but somehow it didn't sound quite as devastating as it had when he'd practiced it in the mirror, and he quietly replaced the receiver in the cradle and considered giving Space a jingle instead.

History was always trying to fatten Time and Time was always trying to rewrite History. At the moment that this happened, everyone sleeping dreamed they were eating vanilla ice cream made by a ball-bearing manufacturer, and with every lick they chipped their teeth.

After God, Time dated a doctor with a God complex and they had all the same problems, though he was a little easier to break up with. "Time waits for no man, is that how it is?" he spat at her between belts of bourbon.

A hundred years after Time's sister died, Time thought she saw Emily sitting in a sidewalk café, drinking an iced drink and eating a sandwich in a way that looked very familiar, but the closer she got to her, the more difficult it was to see her, until Time was standing before a table that appeared unoccupied. Time had often thought of asking God if he could bend the rules for her, if she could just once hold Emily's hand again in hers, only for a second, maybe chauffeur her pneuma around on the handlebars of her bicycle as when they were girls, but she knew he'd never agree to it. What few people knew about God was that he is secretly frightened of revenants, holy or otherwise.

The previous month, two significant things had occurred: an inoculation for the disease that killed Time's sister was developed and a temporal cosmonaut in Russia traveled back in time to visit Peter the Great and upon his return to the present he brought with him a lock of hair that DNA evidence confirmed had indeed been plucked from the head of the czar (while the cosmonaut was there, Peter the Great also practiced his budding dentistry skills on him and he now had a gaping hole in his smile to prove it). But then strange things began to happen. Ten thousand hirsute men living in St. Petersburg all went suddenly bald on the same day; the blue diadem butterflies of Senegal refused to flap their wings and began to disappear; cabinets of wonder full of misshapen men and women and fetal pigs began appearing overnight across Europe and Asia and long queues of people who felt guilty about their curiosity but powerless not to slake it snaked through the cities for miles; and a global potato famine prompted a run on sugar beets and a series of mysterious garottings on trains traveling to the Urals that became known as the Vodka Murders.

Time, who can, when she wants, sprint faster than the naked eye can see, swiped from the research lab a syringeful of the inoculation for her sister's disease, and she found the cosmonaut and ordered him to take her back to her childhood, which he was all too happy to do, he was her biggest fan, he knew her work backwards and forwards, did she know how long he'd been waiting to meet her? oh, of course she did! he laughed and reddened. She asked him to take her to a summer night when she and her sister were chasing fireflies in the backyard, and there Time suddenly was, the tire swing twisting on its rope beside her, and there was Emily, holding a blinking net in the air, catching the light she hoped to tame, and Time held Emily's other hand in hers and it felt cool and smooth like a decorative soap. Emily smiled, then Time quickly jabbed the needle into her sister's eight-year-old arm, but when she did, that simple felicity Time so loved to see slid down Emily's face like rain on a window and Time's clothes began to unravel and fly apart at the seams and the earth growled like a large dog and raised its hackles beneath them.

And then God appeared suddenly (which always gave her the jimjams and had been another bone of contention between them), and he sprayed Time with dry ice and froze her in place. He gently moved her hand, careful not to break it off, so the needle withdrew from her sister's arm, and then he exhaled a thawing sirocco and Time stirred, but she was so startled to see God standing next to her red Radio Flyer wagon she stabbed the needle into his abdomen and pressed the plunger.

Turns out the vaccine for Emily's disease was also an antidote to divinity, and God shrank to the volume of a boy and ran through the hedges, and a faint, unidentifiable din shook the air and bridal bliss calla lilies sprang from the patch of earth God had been standing on. God was never seen by Time again.

Time began to wobble and Emily was no longer beside her, and she thought: *the future is not what it used to be*, it had been altered, and she felt an absence open up in her own history, a revision, a loss, but then she looked at the night sky as she often did to bring her out of the spins and this is what she saw: she saw the winking death that is Emily, that long ago extinction that is burning bright evidence of a stratospheric future, and she felt less afraid.

When God grew up, he did what he'd wanted to do since before he could remember: he engineered and conducted trains, a beautiful orchestration of brute movement, how he'd always imagined God, had there been one. When he came home at night, he kissed his beautiful wife, and for that tender eternity, the spheres orbited and sang, all sleeping people dreamed they hung by their feet suspended from a well-meaning hand the size of the moon, and then the world stopped bleeding and Time felt animal and blameless, a little less fatal, if only for a moment.

Kathryn Dunlevie, *Big Ben,* archival inkjet print on panel

My Dear Emma

*I have just read your letter over again for the fifth time, my own
Dear Emma....*
— Charles Darwin to Emma Wedgwood (Darwin)

*May not the habit in scientific pursuits of believing nothing till
it is proved, influence your mind too much in other things which
cannot be proved in the same way, and which if true are likely
to be above our comprehension . . . . I should be most unhappy if I
thought we did not belong to each other forever.*
— Emma Darwin to Charles Darwin

In the late afternoon light the autumn grass
   is turning gold, a wind stirs in the distant leaves
      with some semblance of waking.

Too often the unimagined contains us, the cool
   weight of evening in the fields
      like sheeted snow. *This is the question:*

Marry (?) Children — (if it please God) —
   Constant Companion . . . who will feel
      interested in one . . . — better than a dog . . . .

Not Marry (?) Freedom to go where one liked . . . —
   Conversation of clever men at clubs — Not forced
      to visit relatives . . . — Then how should I

manage . . . my business if I were obliged to go . . .
   walking with my wife. –Eheu! I never
      should know French . . . or go up in a balloon . . . .

We are always at the edge, a pondering shore
    lapping, lapping, lapping near the deeper
        malaise of the sea, an interval

between. Failure, the day's events, the granite
    compass of time, all the splendors
        of complaint, fiddleheads unfurling

in the brakes. You are so wise
    in your untidiness. It's such a messy world,
        Miss Slip-Slop, a plum tree trailing up

to the eaves, the milliner's bill, kettles
    and saucepans, we are guests waking
        in unfamiliar rooms, the smell of moss

in the gray soul of a pot, a beetle hidden
    in the apple's heart. Today I thought of you
        weeding among the flowerbeds, the small

heated winds of August, every frail stem
    trumpeting upward a brilliant blue, doves
        murmuring the weight of the lost: geological

reasonings, useless appendages, elongated
    femurs, fossils, cowslips and primroses through
        the leaden gaze of ages, past the fields

with their dreams of perfect order, pebbles ground
    until they glitter, whatever herbaceous forms
        flower into . . . *My own dear Emma —*

Transmutation

The more I think, the more convinced I am, that extinction *plays greater part then* transmutation. *— Do species* migrate & die *out?* —
In the place where any species is most common, we need not look for change, ... & this would look like fresh Creation. the gardener separates a plant he wishes to vary—domesticated animals tend to vary.

—Charles Darwin from Notebook E

Gathering, deleting, it's an odd
gentleness, the next of kin, the kinless,
the formless taking form still sings
for those with ears to listen.
The buzzard consuming what's left.
The bee flirting within.
The sap rising again.
— namely how did otter live
Before being made otter.
First one leaf then another.
Blue Jay. Blue Whale. Gray Goose.
Out of the muck comes the mink
and the sinking in between fingers
and toes, claws and fins, the sweep
of an arm, emptiness shuffles
into spaces between. The fleas
embedded on the fleeing goat.
Show me every step between
bull Dog & Greyhound.
Some balance found in the reprobate,
the rotten, the reshaped, the irrevocable
crust stewing in the noon sun.
Seeing from without what's within.
No beeline of fate. 5 will become 6.
In another dark estuary fins become
paws. Too slow to see. A beauty
inconspicuous, nomadic, hidden.
Everything coming to its place
forever. The sheer eloquence

of the overlooked, its fur mangy
and wet and still struggling
up riverbanks. The symmetry of accident.
Of purpose. *Discover*
causes of change. God is in the work.
The gray cliff holds
where pigeons mutter and poop
and step off.

Steve Lautermilch, *Sand Drawing (2+3+2)*, photograph

Listening and Hearing

Some refrain keeps breaking over me,
increasingly luminous with yellow light
so that listening and hearing
                    come in waves of warmth.

The poet says, "Let this line be my last."
Then he hears the soprano reach a higher note,
is unsure how to live there
                    except inside a word.

And a word has another *inside* behind the sound
of being said,
                    a place to stand and breathe—
like a field stumbled onto in the midst of the woods.

Whatever else we call the dandelion fluff sailing
in its own time down the passageways of wind
we might as well agree
                    its motion makes a hymn.

And those monastic scribes, also, writing without
spaces between the words. They must have known
how worship doesn't pause,
                    doesn't reach for punctuation.

Woman Resting

Teotitlán del Valle, Mexico

I have been waiting days to move
to the hammock, to drift
beneath the white portal into a white
dream delineated by black
ink.
     Above me, the green tree
full of green grapefruit and a cluster
of yellow birds. My sky sways
with palm leaves and wingspan.
Footsteps approach
like a lullaby.
        In the distance a child
wails blue syllables and the rooster
releases another *qui-qui-ri-qui-qui.*
I sketch their sounds on paper
alongside the corrugated bray
of burro.
     The hammock swings
in the key of G. I am surrounded by tuning
forks and pomegranate blossoms.
I call this place
Granada.
     Lull is the word that comes
to mind. *Lull* says the wood smoke, *lull*
says the sheet on the line, *lull* says
the loom's shuttle tapping wool strands
of indigo and cochineal
into the snug fit
of weft.

Sometimes the name for gold
dye escapes me, so I put down the pen, feel
the rhythm of my body as if I too
am a leaf lulled by breeze,
as if I too am held to the branch
by a nub of stem.

Steve Lautermilch, *Pine Moon*, photograph

Ode to Spanish

I miss you, Spanish, *te extraño español*; miss meeting you
at the corner where the lottery vendor and the newspaper vendor
compete to see who can shout you out loudest. I miss your everydayness —
our encounters at the cleaners, at the fruit stand, and in recorded telephone
messages. I miss your loudspeaker voice promoting today's political message
or the advantage of *Ariel* over *Fab*, and the knife sharpener's cries, *cuchillos,*
cuchillos, afilo cuchillos, alternating with his whistle. I miss a poet reading his work
on the neighbor's radio and the neighbor's child practicing her English —
poosy cat poosy cat oer av u bean? — the upstairs parrot counting
from one to ten: *uno, dos, tres, cuatro* . . . And the gorgeous cacophony of words
hurled in anger from taxi-cab windows: *¡Pendejo, hijo de puta, cabrón!*

And I miss your songs: *Dame el humo de tu boca* (Give me the smoke from
your mouth). I miss your cadence, your rising at the end of each phrase,
so vowel-happy, so full of yourself, so giddy on rhyme, echoing the rhythm
of a heartbeat, your words bumping into each other, one sentence
sounding like one unending word. And I miss rolling my "r's" around
ferrocarril, my tongue around Nahuatl words like *zempasuchitl, cacahuazintle.*

I miss your taste on my tongue, your music in my mouth.
I miss singing your song.

Fiesta de Semana Santa

On the Final Day of Legal Bullfighting, the Fifth Corrida de
Toros, Easter Sunday, San Antonio, Texas, March 29, 1891

Sueño de Fuego, 5, 584 Kilos,
A Miura Bull from La Ganaderia Miura Lineage

Scratch and snort and huff and puff and put my paw print in
this earth—here is my place and this is my time and all I want
is to fight or fuck, but now I find no cow or steer to my delight so
stomp and spit and huff and thrust, put my rut right in this queer
beast here—six leggies, three armies, two heads—you who've
come to muscle me and make me your morsel but I want you more,
so I drive my horn straight through your torso, and you barb my
hide but I lift you off the earth and shift my hump and dump you
on your back and tear your insides out and stomp and bellow,
grumble and dig and suffer as you die.

Jabbed and hooked four men today and drove them
yellow-hide and sissy-wise away, they barbed me but I drove them
each away—now comes their god, skin like mirrored lights, who
cries and spins and shouts and stamps and hides behind a bright
red cape—it's so fluid each time I move to it I make a crash and
spin and fall—yet it goes swishy sway and ripples like heifer scruff
when I mount and huff and puff and grunt my calf-make rut—and
the red is also me running from my snoring snout—and the cape
goes wiggle waggle more—I rake my hoof and miss my mark again
and grunt and puff and huff and thrust my horn twice more in
earth, holes each the size of this god's waist—about me roars the
horde who wave their small white rags and shriek for ears and
tail—*Toro*, he cries and *Toro*, again—and my wind blows out the
holes in me and so too goes my blood—I cannot lift my head and
I am bone rattled and beaten, defeated in my battle—and now my
nape lies smooth, my tense muscles unknot—I'll soon be leaving
this body behind, rise over the moon to the Great Hot Pasture to
join my harem where my grazing long-lashed gals will swoon and
low when they gaze at me and raise their swishy-tails.

Toro, he calls, and though my mouth is slick with blood, I will
not show my tongue, nor shake the sticks stuck near my spine; no,

let them whistle till their lips go numb: I will not bristle and scratch
at dirt no more nor snore nor snort nor warn nor bluff, but wait till
time is mine and true and ripe with proof, and then, horns low, I
will charge.

❊ ❊ ❊

Ignacio Lopez y Avaloz, 31, 64 kilos,
Famed Matador from Valencia, Spain

I urge the bull to meet my half-cocked thrust and bravely
die same as he fought but now he balks and so we stare like the
last two lovers alive, each facing death without the other: Oh
Lord, bring this noble beast to rest before my feet and tonight I
will spread Your word to the heathen women of this New World,
passing my tongue through their plump lips as if they were plucked
rose petals pressed between the pages of Your book. *Toro, Toro*, I
call, yet he does not move, though I have twisted him in pass upon
pass, spinning blood from his hump to freckle the ochre earth,
packed hard as my cock I sacrifice to virgins who come nightly to
cool my nerves, which thrum as did the organs of La Catedral de
Santa María when I was a babe and wiry and ill-behaved, wrig-
gling in Mama's lap, and the music bellowed through the open
mouths of pipes as large as lances and I would shriek, a sound lost
amid the din, and she would rub my face with the soft skin of her
hands yet deny me suckle again and again and I'd cry the more
demanding milk, my earnest hunger never filled. I set my jaw and
stamp my foot and holler yet again,
　　Toro! The drums roll and the horns swell and the bull comes
and I cross before him, sword straight out, but he swings his head
at me and unbinds me from the earth and my mouth goes dry as si-
lenced organ pipes and the world becomes a singular hiss, as when
Mary's milk missed the saint's lips and scalded on a searing stone,
and I smack against the ground and the air explodes from my lungs
and back and a fire burns riot through my guts while I try to suck
and suck and suck and suck—

❊ ❊ ❊

Michael Garriga

Witness: Jose "Pepe" Hernandez, 33, 61 Kilos,
Ignacio's Mozo de Estoques from Priego de Cordoba, Spain

Ignacio poses before this bull like St. George above his dragon and he lays the Toledo steel estoque across the blood-red muleta, which the wind catches and raises and flaps, exposing his thighs—I should have soaked the flannel cape, put more water weight on its hem against this whipping wind that burns a chill across my nape, though a moment ago I warmed to his *paso doble*: the man and his cape and the bull in his cape formed a statue, brief and sublime, that spun painfully slow and tight, the blood of the bull brushed a bright streak across the gold-threaded buttons, which I fastened for Ignacio not two hours before, when I'd sewn him into his pants and plaited his hair, pinning it beneath his felt montera, and as I knelt before him buffing his shoes, I looked up and saw pity across his eyes, as if he and I had not once competed for top purses until I was gored by a bull who lacked the grace to kill, leaving me instead a cripple who will never fight another bull nor carry the full Fiesta de Semana Santa bier again—the bull charges now and as one mouth the arena gasps and I am a child again in the Caves of Nerja, where the waves would break against the vaulted rocks, the water receding and sucking the air out with it, tugging the breath from my young lungs, and I'd stand shocked-still and numb until the next wave came with cold spray to bring my senses back: the bull has buried his horn hilt-deep in the belly of Ignacio and he is as dead as this bull soon will be—his body will be dragged by horse and heavy rope from plaza to matadero where his head will be removed, hide stripped, meat butchered and shipped to market, and sold to people still mourning the loss of Ignacio, who has toured this outpost a hero of the Old World, and he will have his body hoisted onto the shoulders of toreadors as they bear him to Catedral de San Fernando, where he will lie in repose five days and nights, lit dimly by candle for pilgrims come the world over to kneel by the hundreds and thousands and smear their tears and fingerprints on his glass coffin, covering it, with roses and rosaries, and wail as he is buried in full regalia and people will speak of him in cafés, will read of him every Easter in newspapers, will name their children after him, and he will become the Romero of this New World.

But I will simply sew a black brassard about my right sleeve, a gesture of sorrow, and move to Mexico and search for a new torero, whom I will dress and assist and hold his estoque and muleta, which I will wet so that it is heavy enough to hide him from the eye of the bull—that is, unless he ever disrespects me.

Erica Lehrer, photograph

Trephine

Jolie and Darren followed the asphalt ribbon from the hills into the low-lying Pennsylvanian farmland. It was the furthest south Jolie had ever been. She adjusted her position in the back-seat, scratched the dog's head, and smoothed the blankets on her lap. She'd been on the road with Darren for six months. Before that, after her release, she'd rented a clean and warm trailer that sat in the back field of an old farm; the farmhouse roof peeked over a division of trees, the chimney sputtering clouds of woodsmoke on cold evenings. The farmer's widow only charged her fifty dollars a month. Each morning, Jolie awoke with the dawn, pleased to stare through the window as the sun bloomed over the grass, the trees, the long fallow fields engulfed with foxglove and aster and holly-hock. She followed the movements of the crows as they marked ever-shifting boundaries with simple language. But that was before Darren broke his parole by robbing a Hallmark, where he'd gone to buy her a birthday gift.

She'd known him for a few brief months, and although she hadn't been smitten by his looks or his dim attentions, he wasn't mean and he demanded nothing and required little, so she spent a few nights a week with him, when she wasn't waiting tables. On the day in question, Jolie agreed to stay in the car so that whatever he bought would be a surprise. Inside, he saw the cash drawer sluice open. Those green bills all flat and orderly trapped his atten-tion in a mystical trawl and he'd had little choice but to follow the dictates of his nature. Back in the car, he'd tried to justify his ac-tions in an excited, incoherent jabber. Please, Jolie said, just drive.

She missed her little trailer immediately, knew it was gone forever. Darren had a felony record and had done two years for breaking and entering. Consorting with former or current feloni-ous persons violated the stipulations of her parole. That afternoon, she spent an hour with her head on a swivel, sure she'd see the flashing lights pulsing in the encroaching dusk, sure she'd be wear-ing a jumpsuit before dawn. But as it happened, Darren was adept at these small larcenies and her contribution to their continuing spree—simply waiting in the car and planning the escape route— seemed innocent. Darren's dream was to raise hunting dogs but he lost track of that goal when they spied vulnerable knick-knack

shops or fruit stands or candle stores in tourist towns, or, like today, a scrapbooking store called Forget-me-Not.

She sat in the back seat with the dog, waiting for Darren. It
was all part of the deal; she didn't want to be directly implicated
in any new crimes. Although he was gone only a few moments,
she grew instantly sleepy. She closed her eyes and had a quick,
vivid dream of cotton candy—mounds and mounds of it, fluffy and
pink, dissipating on her tongue. She woke after what seemed like
a long time to Darren opening the door. They'd parked around the
corner from the store, tucked in between two large SUVs. Darren stripped away his mask, caught his breath, and changed his
sweatshirt. Jolie consulted her map. They waited for the shock
of the robbery to dull into a nervous acceptance. When the police
arrived, Darren pulled the car around the block and they'd driven
away like any number of other cars crowding the street.

❊ ❊ ❊

Later, after an hour driving through cornfields bordered by
split-rail fencing, Darren broke the silence. How you doing back
there? he said.

I'm hungry, Jolie said. So's Randolph.

Me, too. Let's stop.

Go a bit further, go another fifteen miles. I'll be okay. I wish
it wasn't so late. I'm in the mood for an Egg McMuffin.

At these words, Randolph perked his ears. Three months
ago, they found him sitting at the intersection of two busy roads,
as if waiting for a bus, and when Darren stopped at the light, Jolie
opened the door and the dog stood slowly and stiffly, wagging its
tail. Come on, she'd said. She patted the seat and he climbed in.
She appreciated his chucklehead, his bony and solid mass sharing
the backseat, but she worried about his former owners, and some
small girl crying into her pillow over her long-lost dog.

Randolph knows the words Egg McMuffin, Jolie said.

Of course he does, Darren said. He's no dummy.

If she were to leave this dog by the side of the road, he'd
survive, wind up in a better car, with better owners. Darren, on
the other hand, would be hopeless and lost, returning to the same
towns over and over, committed to his thievery until he was arrested and remanded to the state penitentiary. It was Jolie who

tracked the stores and towns, who kept them focused and sustainable. Several times, they'd stopped for a few weeks and it was Jolie who worked. Darren had never held down a job longer than a couple of paychecks and his interest in work hovered like a hazy fantasy, quickly burning off in the light of each day. The money was Jolie's department, too. She'd opened an account at Bank of America and set aside a bit of each payday—legal or not—for deposit. Now, she had seven hundred dollars beneath the underwear in the pack, too much to carry. The weight of it made her nervous. As they drove into a small town, she saw the bank sign. Pull over, she said, I got to make a deposit.

She never worried about Darren robbing anything so large as a bank; he knew his limitations. Banks were bright and unforgiving, like churches. Here, the tables were turned and Darren sat in the car while Jolie went inside. I don't trust them crooks, he said.

❊ ❊ ❊

Next morning, they drove into Gettysburg. Darren went into McDonald's to buy breakfast. When Jolie was a child, her mother had cleaned offices at night. When she finished near dawn on Saturday morning, she'd come home and rouse her daughter. They'd scrub their faces clean and put on dresses and pull their hair away from their faces and when they walked into McDonald's, Jolie felt like her mother owned the restaurant, like they weren't the people they were. They ordered Egg McMuffins and square hash browns and orange juice or hotcakes with dipping cups of butter-flavored syrup. And, oh, what a beautiful woman her mother was, sharp shoulders rising from her dress, chin high, clean hair still slick from washing held back with Bobby pins, a few loose strands drooping across her ears like tinsel. They ate at other places too, mom-and-pop diners mostly, but Jolie never felt fully comfortable sitting in their high-backed booths or their patched vinyl chairs or eating from their heavy plates piled high with layers of meat and mashed potatoes with lumpy gravy encroaching the overcooked vegetables or ordering from waitresses whose fingers fluttered against the shoulders or wrists of regular customers.

Darren's robberies didn't feel particularly immoral compared with her crime. She'd served her sentence—eight years—but forgiveness was another matter. On Sundays, her mother had taken her to church, but it was so long ago that Jolie could recall the building only in the gauziest of abstractions: four white walls racing toward the ceiling; the altar a willowy way-station bedecked in swaths of red and white; Jesus in wretched pain looming above it all. On most days, Jolie rarely thought of Matthew, her husband, or of the moment in which she shot him dead. After the arrest and during her trial, she often went to the jail's chapel and, although she'd sat on the folding chairs and talked to one or the other of the rotating ministers in the pale room with a gray floor that also housed AA meetings on Tuesdays and Thursdays, she'd never once found relief nor solace. After her conviction, in prison, the chapel had long hard benches, a permanent and sturdy cross bolted to the cinderblock wall, and a more singular purpose. Many inmates attended church and claimed to have unearthed a redemptive message, but nothing dimmed Jolie's longing for a more permanent release of her relief. For that is indeed what Matthew's death brought—relief. She was glad he was dead and she was glad she was the one who'd killed him. How could one explain such a thing?

When Darren came around the corner of the McDonald's, he skipped over the curb and waved as he bounced through the bushes that divided the drive-through lane from the rear side parking lot. Not until later would she realize that he had no paper bag of food, no tray of beverages. Give me my egg sandwich, she said, fingers entwined, hopeful.

It was too late.

Too late? she said. It's not eleven o'clock.

They closed down breakfast early.

They're a franchise, Jolie said. They can't make their own rules.

The presumed flouting of the franchise structure distracted her. The lack of their usual routine—handing food back and forth, pouring creams into their coffees—confused her. Randolph sat alert, nose glistening. Darren wasn't offering anything; he was just driving with purpose, the way she'd taught him, moving along a series of smaller residential roads. When Jolie leaned over the seat, she saw the bank bag. Darren's ski mask lay on the seat, a dark stain.

* * *

Darren drove for thirty minutes until Jolie saw the lot near the statue of the soldier and the historical placard. Darren turned into the small, shady parking area and drove the car behind a tall hedge. We have to ditch this car, Jolie said.

Maybe they didn't see? The manager was pretty scared. They were all scared.

Someone saw. We have to get out now, camp for the night.

They took their packs and walked to the road and past the statue. The sunlight glossed the soldier's shoulders and all was still except for the insects buzzing and droning. They started across the field. Randolph trotted along behind them. Darren carried the tent, Jolie the food and money. The bank bag was three thousand dollars heavy. She took large strides, paddled her arms against the switch grass and Queen Anne's lace. Darren struggled to keep up, puffing and panting and sweating and stumbling.

Jolie, he said, this pack is heavy.

Not as heavy as mine, she said.

Can you slow down just a bit?

You don't have to come with me, Jolie said.

But Darren was there to stay. The cooking pots and the little gas stove rattled around in his pack. Both of them were wearing sweatshirts too heavy for the warm day. Soon, rings of perspiration marked their collars and their armpits, but Jolie did not slow down. When the field opened onto a road, she stepped onto the blacktop and quickened her pace yet again. At the next crossroad, she followed a sign pointing toward a campsite. She kept to the shoulder and her shoes scuffed a dusty, disquieting cloud. The pack straps dug into her shoulders. Soon, she was a hundred yards ahead of Darren, with Randolph in the no-man's-land between. The muscles in her thighs grew taut and stiff, but still she pressed on, sucking down rancorous, insufficient draughts of hot afternoon air.

❊ ❊ ❊

Once, after her mother was arrested, a deputy came at three o'clock in the morning on a hot July night to fetch Jolie. His insistent knocking had drawn her from a sweaty sleep, sheets kicked completely off the bed. She'd seen him before, around town, in the school for safety day, at the side of the road directing traf-

fic for road crews. He looked down through the screen like Jolie
was nothing and the things in their house just trash—dirty, worn
thin, broke-down, patched. A colony of moths flapped and droned
against the screendoor and battered themselves against the porch
light.

I'm sorry to bother you, he said, but your mother isn't coming
home tonight. She's okay, but she had a little too much to drink
and wasn't feeling too good, so we're keeping her with us. She was
calling for you, but we can't let you into the jail and we can't let
you stay here. Do you have anywhere you can go? Anyone you can
call?

I can stay here, Jolie said.

I can't let you stay here by yourself, he said.

I stay here all the time, Jolie said. I stay here every night. I
make breakfast in the mornings.

Maybe a neighbor? Who takes care of you?

Jolie latched the door. She wasn't afraid. She'd felt the opposite of fear—a surging pulse of anger—and she'd locked the
door for him. She was certain that if he tried to come in, she'd bite
him hard, or scratch his eyes. The center of her palms itched as he
jiggled the door handle. What about your daddy? he said. Does he
live here in town?

He doesn't live anywhere, Jolie said.

Grandma? Aunt? Someone watches you, right? A friend of
the family?

If you open that door, Jolie said, I'll call the cops.

Aw, come on, little girl. I'm tired too. Your mother was no
picnic, all right?

I'll scream. I'll do worse than scream. You'll be sorry.

The deputy was slight, but with a roll of fat over his belt that
reminded Jolie of a Life Saver. He was sweating through his shirt.
He fluttered a hand near his ears to keep away the mosquitoes.
His badge glistened in the porch light and the tapping of his shoe
against the porch decking contributed a hollow, lonely rhythm to
the night.

I'm going to have to call social services, he said.

Do what you have to do, Jolie said.

No one ever came. Maybe the deputy couldn't rouse the
right person, or maybe he just wanted to go home and she slipped
through some administrative crack. Her mother was home by

ten the next morning, hungover but whole. She found Jolie eating spoonfuls of peanut butter and jelly straight from the jar and drinking lime Kool-Aid from the pitcher. She rubbed her daughter's head and apologized for acting so dumb and then she went to soak in the tub for a long time. Later, since the car had been impounded, they walked into town for lunch. Down Route One, cars zooming by on either side, radios blasting, voices from open windows layered into the cloud of exhaust—they walked hellbent for McDonald's. Once there, Jolie was allowed a Big Mac just for herself. While they ate, Jolie's mother cast her furious eyes on the other patrons, who gave the dusty and tired pair a wide berth.

✳ ✳ ✳

They pitched their tents near a troop of Boy Scouts who spent much of the afternoon running into and out of a cornfield that bordered the campsite. Being near the boys felt like camouflage, but Jolie was nervous about being stationary.

We can't just sit around, she said. We don't want people to recognize us.

How they going to recognize us? Darren said.

Maybe the people here were in the restaurant. Did you think of that?

They studied the other campsites—twelve or so, all told, packed into a little community. At one, near the end of the lane, smoke gathered above the fire pit in a flat, motionless cloud.

Okay then, Darren said. Let's go look at statues.

They used a long rope to tie Randolph to the picnic table and filled a bowl of water. Jolie gave him a treat and worried the loose skin at the top of his head.

He's all right, Darren said. It isn't like you won't see him in a few hours.

I know, Jolie said. But he's a good dog.

Before leaving the campsite, she stopped to talk to one of the Scouts. He was a scrawny little boy with scratches all along his face from running and falling in the field. As the other boys came from and returned to the trampled corn, the boy sat on the ground with a canteen in his lap. He was so pale that Jolie leaned down and touched his arm to make sure he wasn't feverish. You see my dog over there? she said.

The boy nodded.

I'll give you ten dollars now and ten dollars when I get back if you watch him as best you can. Will you do that for me?

Yes, ma'am, the boy said. But I have to go on a hike later.

What is your name?

Jimmy, the boy said.

Well, Jimmy, if you go on a hike, will you make sure his water dish is full? He's an awfully thirsty dog.

I can do that, the boy said.

Jolie put the bill in his hand and he looked at it as if he'd never seen that much money. His eyes were red and watery. She instantly wanted to give him all the money and the dog, to steal him and take him to her little trailer on the farm with the smoke rising from the farmhouse chimney and the morning sun coming in through the windows dim at first and then bright, to hold him like a mother close to her heart, to feed him Big Macs and fries, to sing to him as they worked together in a small garden, to survive until he was an adult and off on his own and not succumb quietly to cancer, to not leave, ever. But those thoughts rattled in and out of the basket, shaken loose by more urgent requirements.

❊ ❊ ❊

Soldiers had died everywhere at Gettysburg, over fifty thousand men. It didn't seem possible, or real, despite the written and photographic evidence presented at nearly every turn. Men died in cornfields—perhaps even the cornfield that the Boy Scouts were flattening—on roads, in drainage ditches and trenches, on bridges, in water, running up hills, running down. In the visitor center, dozens of displays testified to the horrible reality. In one glassy case, Civil War era surgical equipment lay in orderly, sanitized rows, ready for use—saws and pliers and hammers and, most sobering of all, the trephine drills that bored into wounded soldier's skulls to release pressure on the brain. It was a simple apparatus: a hollow, cylindrical saw blade the same diameter as a quarter, attached to the end of a short post with a wooden handle. The simplicity magnified an alarming ferocity; its tiny teeth snarled in the clear vitrine light. At another display, she learned what each soldier carried, including the weight of the equipment. Fifty or sixty pounds each, she said, they must have been so strong.

Or tired, Darren said. Tired kids in the wrong place at the wrong time.

They walked towards the area where Pickett charged and lost his men, thousands of dead and wounded. The undulating fields rose toward a stone wall and a small copse of trees, the grass hazy and yellowing in the late afternoon sun. Jolie resisted contemplating the once blood-soaked soil. It must have been wall-to-wall bodies, she said. I bet you could cross the fields without touching the ground.

At the copse, looking across the battlefield, Jolie wondered just how she'd got to this exact spot. She thought: what has transpired in my life that I should be here, of all places, so far from where I started? Other tourists studied the plaques, ran their hands over the stubbly stems of the cannons, took pictures of the rows of grassy hillocks that could have been anywhere, except for the weight of what had been borne and lost there. The day's suffocating light dispersed itself over every surface equally.

❉ ❉ ❉

The Boy Scouts were loud and gangly and insomniac and Jolie slept but little despite her weary limbs. Her shoulders ached and her legs twitched. The boy she'd asked to watch Randolph was nowhere to be found, though the dog was fine. In the dark of the tent, she began to wonder if she had imagined the whole exchange, yearned the boy into existence. In the morning, they were awake to see dawn burnish the undamaged cornstalks. Darren was morning-quiet and Jolie checked her packing list twice, three times, balancing her strict orderliness with hurried efficiency. The Boy Scouts were beginning to stir as Darren and Jolie lifted packs onto their shoulders. They crunched their way through the gravel parking lot and onto the main road. A patchy fog hovered in the ditches and seamed its way through the scrubby trees and stone walls. They walked single file, with Darren taking the lead. The road lay straight and flat and the sun burned the air clear and the heat gathered in their armpits and sweat dripped down their backs, until Jolie felt as if she was marching into battle ill-prepared and hopeless. The morning traffic began its crawl and the hunger raced through her body, swelled in her stomach before being flung in all directions. Where in the world could they possibly eat?

After several hours, they found an old Chevette at the out-
skirts of a visitor parking lot. It seemed to have no owner, or no
immediate prospects of an owner, so Darren applied his know-
ledge of ignitions to the dusty wires beneath the steering column
and soon they were driving again. Jolie piloted them straight
away from Gettysburg. The emptiness was awful and she missed
every McDonald's she'd ever been to in her whole life—the smell
of grease, the red and yellow tables, the coffee so hot it was like
drinking your own tiny piece of the sun—the whole damn mess.

Matthew had refused her McDonald's. He didn't like their
fish, he said, or the workers or the color of the uniforms. That's
what she remembered most about him; not his fists, not being
pushed down a flight of stairs, not being locked in the closet as a
punishment for forgetting laundry, not the unsavory aggressive-
ness in the bedroom or the phantom jealousies or the routine name-
calling or the sense of self-loathing she underwent each time she
swore to leave and reneged. Of all those things, what rankled most
was not being able to eat what she wanted. Bruises faded, but that
appetite found her each day, like a dirty finger in a wound. She
could never pinpoint for anyone—judge, jury, lawyers—what the
final straw had been. Perhaps there had been no final straw, just a
long simmering stew finally reaching its boil.

They'd lived near the far edge of the county. After she was
sure he was dead, she got into his truck and drove to town and
went to McDonald's. She sat right in the front window, the Golden
Arches looming like a child's drawing of mountains, like a yel-
low-brick road. Several police cruisers pulled into the parking lot.
The policemen were in no hurry. They stood next to their cars and
chatted, pulled off their hats and wiped their hands across their
foreheads, blue synthetic fabric uniforms pulsing in the heat of the
day, arms slick with sweat. These were the same young men who
would respond to her call, nearly two hours later, after she'd eaten
all she could eat and had returned home. All was as she'd left it.
Matthew lay in the living room, one arm crooked under his head as
if he were merely napping. The rooms of the house were silent and
still to the point of airlessness, just like the battlefield, full of ghosts
and regret and weight she couldn't tally.

❊   ❊   ❊

The Chevette rattled and shook every time Darren tried to push it past sixty. They drove nearly three hours without speaking. Jolie had stopped giving directions and Darren just drove up and down one mountain after another. Sunlight trumpeted through the windows, followed by long bouts of sobering shadow. Jolie pinched her eyes as the familiar hunger bored her clean, releasing those packed away and unbearable images of her mother's final sick days that arrived so quickly and offered little time for mourning. After her death, social services arrived to whisk Jolie away to a foster home. She had no problem with her foster family — she could no longer recall their names — but swirled through those months mostly mocus, frenzied one moment, lethargic the next, spacy and weeping nearly all the time. For her fourteenth birthday, she'd run away. By sixteen, she'd met Matthew. By eighteen was a convicted murderer. Only a jury sympathetic to the photos of the bruises on her back and shoulders and the litany of Matthew's abuses kept her from being imprisoned far longer. Now, still not thirty, the balance of her life lay forward, not backward, but it was a doomed march toward an unattainable copse along a ridge defended by superior forces, led by a general unsure of his approach. Outside, a long and green valley stretched before the car.

Where are we? she said.

West Virginia, Darren said.

That's too far.

How do you mean?

You need to let me out, Jolie said.

What do you mean let you out?

I can't do it. I can't stay.

Because I robbed a McDonald's?

Yes.

But Darren didn't stop driving and Jolie didn't say anything as she counted the mile markers. Her maps were useless. Each unknown mile brought her farther from any place she'd ever known. Stop the car, she said.

I can't do that, he said. We're in the middle of nowhere.

I feel for you, for the dog, for all of it, Jolie said, but I need to get out.

Maybe we can try a Wendy's. Be honest, Egg McMuffins aren't worth all this fuss.

It's not about the goddamn Egg McMuffins. Jolie couldn't tell if she was yelling or whispering. The wind roared against the windows. The little car shook and rattled and whined. Randolph stirred at the mention of food, but he only raised his head a bit from his paws and then resettled. Darren's eyes were drawn and bagged, puffy orbs of exhaustion in the rear-view mirror. He braked his way down a long, sloping switchback. Below them, the valley floor was dotted with Monopoly-sized houses and shimmering ponds the size of silver dollars. The view was clear and the valley broken into orderly grids. Jolie wasn't sure of her geography, but perhaps she was looking at the beginnings of the Great Plains. Perhaps they were coming to a long unmapped prairie.

Take this money, Jolie said.

She dug the bank bag from her pack and tossed it onto the front seat.

What do you want me to do with this?

Either take it and let me out or drive back, Jolie said.

And do what?

Return the money.

They'd arrest me.

You don't have to go in. I'll do it. I'll take it in and find the manager and apologize. I'll do it all. I just can't have it here. I can't breathe.

Darren pulled over to the shoulder and turned around. West Virginia and the remaining states, uncharted and undiscovered, stirred in Jolie a lonesomeness as simple and sharp as the teeth on the trephine drill.

What is it? Darren said.

Just go back.

All the way to Gettysburg?

He pointed at what lay beyond the rear window, his long finger connected to all she'd left behind. He needed only to crook a delicate knuckle to reel her home, to instigate a return. Jolie took his hand with both of hers. She was suffused with an empty and fathomless craving.

Yes, she said, that way. The sooner you go back, the sooner we can eat.

We Could Blow This Place Up if We Wanted To

While we're still young, let's blow kisses,
our brains out, leave molars behind grinding
on the ground. I need love tough, and you're one cheap
steak, a bona fide pretty needle, who sends me candy
hearts in juicy Rx bottles, *and if love be rough with you—*
be rough with love. And you're banging around below
my windowsill, breaking bottles, working me up till I
rain out my window, a beet-red nerve ending, a bruised
up cherry in night's ear swinging and screaming—
Talk seedy to me, baby! The passion, two far gone
angels nailing crossed hearts up against the crosswalk

where we blew up and dangled bloodshot off the lip
of the river in the wet dreamland grass, feeling the pinch
then pulses from bug bites starting to swell.

Raised by Wolves

Perhaps it was the matching scars we shared
from when our mother would pick us up by our

necks with her teeth, which caused you to tell
the class my twin and me were raised by wolves.

Ms. Bishop, was it nurture or pedigree that made
my twin and me not stop wanting to break things.

You were talking about genetics, how chromosomes
bite like snakes, stain like ink, how cells chip off,

then splinter, red in the womb, like an ingrown
hair. Ms. Bishop, my twin brother was found out

in Algebra during a lesson on roots, how to find
a value for a zero—and maybe it was his tail

that put him in the psych ward where he shuffles,
where he waits, where he looks for us in heaps

of *National Geographics*. I miss him. I miss how
I'd sit on one hill, he on the other and we'd

try to catch each other's echoes with nets. I miss
how when the moon swelled big enough, pieces

would drip down on us, we'd gather the debris
in mason jars, watch the pieces become clear

like rock candy, and Ms. Bishop, you need to know
our mother was never buried alive. She left in

the morning when I was sitting on the couch,
drinking fruit punch from a cereal bowl and,

for the first time, she asked to do my hair. It was
hailing outside, but the windows had their mouths

open, and I watched the squirrels get pulverized,
and when cars in driveways started to look like

pockmarked teens, my mother took my last
knot out, and pulled so hard I thought my scalp

would unwind from my head, and lie ghost
on the floor, swim spineless like a jellyfish,

but instead the hail got louder, then a window
broke. My twin and I were left electric splashes

of static, but we were cared for by Mars who left us
flickering on the welcome mat of the wolf household,

where, yes, we were raised, and I'm going to wait
right here in this kennel with all the other tattooed

children, who lap up heartfelt bowls of rock candy,
rain and crumbs of moonlight.

Michael DeRosa, *Wolf: Instinctual Behavior,*
acrylic on canvas, 11" x 14"

HONORABLE MENTION
PATRICIA HAWLEY

Transmutation

I am a house of silver twigs,
this delicate mass
of balanced atoms, genes,
whose pulsing streams of blood
once rushed with mine,
is my child—
my heart's twin—
born feathered, winged,
ready to leave me.
I am transformed,
refuge for birds in winter.

These Funerals of Old Friends

Hearse turns in crow circle
to the front.
Even if
expected,
each loss
siphons my lungs dry.
Those of us left
embrace,
curved like bears in caves,
waiting out winter,
dreaming
of, perhaps, nothing, or
lick of honey on lips,
buzzing rasp
of a phalanx of bees,
sweet dank of leaves
released from frost,
raspberries
hot in sun.

From the collection of the Managing Editor, photograph

Her Tattooed Back

Lord, are not my sister's wings
beautiful in the golden gloss
of hospital lights?

Shoulder blade anchored fans
of splayed feathers
(neither white nor ethereal)
but blood-red as a harlot's cheek —
at each wing-tip a tiny death star.

I believe
You must have ached over
each defiant tattoo
dyed during the dark years
she charred the hillsides with fire.

Or did her fierce voice
in the wilderness redeem?

This woman — never an angel,
nor saint —
but human who
fed one-legged beggars,
touched our lepers hopeful of
miraculous healing.

Tonight, when I whisper   *Judith*

feathers ruffle
to the oil on my fingers
as she pauses on death's limb,
now only a wing-beat

away from the quickening, forgiveness,
Your ever-lasting light.

The Body's First Lessons

Every day millions
of cells, saucers too small to see,
spin away into the infinite,

reducing us a breath at a time
and with every kiss.
From the first

childhood tooth string-looped,
we are unbodied
piece by piece:

strand of hair, fish-hook reefed
on sweater sleeve,
silent bones dissolving into chalk

guyed by wire and hinge.
We witness sweat's T-shape
between breasts and over brow.

Menses. Blood from a thorn.
Barbed wire. An envelope cut
to the tip of the tongue.

Even these clipped fingernails,
luminous seeds
tossed to a devouring ground.

This disintegrating house.

from *Phantom Hour*

> *O Memory!*
> —Abraham Lincoln

The more I try to hurt
the more I participate in making
a cavity in the chest
weaker with each palpitation.
Wired up with nowhere to go
but back to the hospital.
The records show the genetic disposition,
a history we can't modify, really.
We can see all the way to where
the sea and sky dissolve in haze
white snow or clouds or
maybe the white of someone's heaven.
It's anyone's guess.
Say it's just the thin veil of consciousness
or say a tendon holding this life
to this moment
or an unsound bridge with an exit
for each relation's roadside hamlet.
Here is a rabbit raised for stew.
Here, gradually, the past makes the heart
more reliant on futurity
than what the trobar* might sing.

* a form of light lyric poetry employed by troubadours

+

I was the cat's meow, he says. There is a humor in this statement, but it is sad and reminiscent. The cat's meow, he says. My grandfather, he says, was a twin. James Early was. His brother was Henry Lee, named for the famous Revolutionary War general. I was not an animal's call to attention. I was not present at the Leipzig Debate, 1519. I am not a daughter of the Revolutionary War. Still, war is why this is an American story. Why the name was sold to the British Army for a king's pocket full of coin. No sooner did the Hessian soldier come in contact with German-American citizens than he deserted the ranks on the other side of Ashley River. He found a safe opportunity in German settlements in the Carolinas. There they spake the German language and bore their German names. This is why the name spread throughout the place like a ministry. This second Edict of Worms. This is where my name comes from, and so your name, he says. It is a strong name. It is the way we are connected. It has wandered here. It is the sound a cat makes.

+

A heart goes bad and the mind
misses a beat.
A machine motivates
the organ, in a manner of speaking
which echoes the poem.
It isn't music or science
but a metaphor for familial love
and all its complications.
Flush the misfiring muscle.
Flesh born of your flesh.
Found our name on a small church.
The bad heart of our history.
Here is the body, and here the blood.
These are what we take, what
we know of the world's rhythm.
Here is a stone for the family plot
for those whose bodies and stones
now rest beneath Lake Murray,
Lexington, South Carolina.
Sacred to the memory it says.
If only, like this, the mind
were a stone
and the story its engraver.

Jolly Old England

I could take him to see *Grand Torino* because he might like the way the character talks, in the mock-bigot language that working men his age used to josh each other. Then again, it might set him off, cause him to start talking like that out loud in front of people who don't know the difference, don't make the distinction between mock and real. And god knows it was hard enough to squelch it in the first place, took more scolding than I want to remember. So I opt instead for the shoot'em-up, the remake of a classic western, *3:10 to Yuma* — with modern special effects, of course, the action carried to absurdity, *Die Hard* done in cowboy clothes.

Besides, it's playing at the cheap theater, only two bucks for a matinee in a slightly run-down old movie house, so maybe he'll feel like it's old times. I always do. But halfway through, he starts talking — I start to shush him, but there are only two other people all the way in the back row who seem way too focused on feeling each other up to give a damn. So I let him talk.

"I don't understand this," he says.

"What?" I whisper.

"The movie."

"What don't you understand?"

"What's going on."

So I explain it, the hero's hungry family about to lose their land, the dangerous outlaw he's trying to take to meet the train to prison because of the reward, the gang shadowing them all the way and attacking what once was a whole posse but now is only the hero and his son. As I talk, it does seem more complicated than I thought. So I leave out the part about the outlaw's moral complexity.

"Oh," he answers. But only ten more minutes pass before he says the same thing again.

"Do you want to go?" I ask.

"Yes," he says.

I like that about him now, his lack of equivocation. He just answers. On the other hand, it makes a simple afternoon less simple. It's only two o'clock, and we've already had lunch. So we get in the truck, and I drive through town aimlessly, asking him where he'd like to go, as if he had a place in mind.

"Little Joe's," he says after I think he's forgotten the question.

"Oh yeah," I tell him, "wish we could. It closed."

"Oh," he says and doesn't even bother to ask when.

We keep moving slowly down Union Street like we're looking for another place just as good, but really I know where we're headed, to the freeway to take him back. I look at him and wonder if he knows it too. His problem seems more about remembering things than thinking about them, and it's easy to forget the difference. Hard to follow a movie plot if you can't remember who the character is or why what's happening now is happening.

Maybe he does know what's happening now because he seems to be looking a block ahead to where the on-ramp is. I can't stand the way I think he looks, so when I see the cheesy sign for the Churchill Arms, complete with a neon Beefeater holding up a pint, I ask him if he wants to stop for a beer. He understands *that* clearly enough.

"Yes," he says without equivocation.

A serving wench opens the door for us, bowing her puffy bonnet. I hate the fantasy she invites us to engage in. Jolly old England, the tourist version. Hate it because I lived there for six months and know the difference.

"We're just here for a quick drink," I tell her a little too tersely when she reaches for menus, so she blinks and her smile seems to harden, and I feel like a jerk. It's not like she made us come in.

"Sorry," I say, "today's been a little tough," and can't help letting my eyes roll toward him. Too easy to do that, so even as her smile softens again, I think I really am a jerk. At least she doesn't try to talk fake Cockney.

"No worries," she says in tinkly Californian. "How 'bout over here?"

"That'd be great," I say with way too much enthusiasm.

There's no one in the bar in the middle of the afternoon, so she seats us at the wooden chess-top table in front of the stone fireplace with a gas fire and concrete logs. This is accidentally accurate. Most pubs can't burn coal or real logs any more. I tell him this for conversation, and he says, "Oh."

Another wench takes our drink order, and we sit with our pints of Bass, smiling at each other like we're enjoying ourselves. And maybe he really is. It's probably just me that needs to keep up the conversation. I must look like it too, because he asks me if I'm bored.

"Oh, no, not at all," I say. "This is nice," and sweep the room with my smile. "Do you remember much about England?"

"Yeah," he says, "I sure do."

"So what do you remember the most about it?"

He pauses only a beat before he says, "The doodlebugs."

"Huh? The what?" I say, so he repeats it.

I smile for real now, picturing some charming detail, a summer picnic in the British countryside.

"What do you remember about them?"

He stops smiling though, searching for a way to tell me about it.

"How they buzzed," he says and thinks about it a while more.

"In the countryside?" I ask, trying to help him bring it back. He looks up like the question's odd.

"Everywhere," he explains. "Then they'd go quiet."

"They would?" I ask because I don't know what to ask. He nods.

"Yeah, and you didn't know where they'd hit. You had to wait till they blew up."

"Oh, oh," I say, realizing where he is now and when, "you're talking about those, what the hell were they called? The German rockets . . .V-2s."

"V-1s," he says without having to pause. "V-2s were later."

"Oh, yeah, right," I say like I know. "That had to be scary as hell."

"Yeah, it was," he says, and I can see him still thinking. "But your mother didn't mind," he adds.

"Mind what?"

"The doodlebugs. She liked it there."

"Oh, uh huh, well actually, Dad, Mom wasn't there when the doodlebugs were," I tell him. It's clear his memory has jumped twenty-five years or so to a trip they took, and I'm about to explain this to him. But he blinks and looks worried now, because he believes me when I tell him about getting mixed up, and this time it clearly bothers him, having to remember the doodlebugs without Mom. And maybe because I've downed my Bass too quick or maybe because I'm just tired of straightening it all out, I think, *What difference does it make? Who cares how he remembers it?*

"Are you sure?" he asks, and I say no. But he's not so sure now and goes on trying to remember it. "She was in the cellar," he says.

"She was?" I say. "What cellar?"

"Where she lived," he says and looks surprised, lowers his head to think about it some more.

"Oh she lived there, huh? In a house?" I'm wondering if he'll put their house in England too and add a cellar. I shouldn't play with his mind, I know, but this has gotten interesting. For once I'm really not bored.

"No," he answers without equivocation, "not a house, a. . ."

"A flat?"

"That's right, a flat, a big brick one." He thinks about it so long I get tired of waiting.

"And it had a cellar?"

"Yeah," he says but doesn't look up. "The sirens went off." He's looking at his beer, remembering.

"And you went down in the cellar?"

"Yeah. She didn't want to, but I made her."

"Why didn't she want to?"

"Her dad wasn't there."

"He wasn't? Where was he?"

"I don't know," he says, "but she cried."

I should stop this. It's gone in a bad direction, and he looks upset. I don't know what details to straighten out so he won't remember Mom crying, take him back to her not minding the doodlebugs. Instead I gesture to the serving wench to break his focus. She brings her perkiness and bonnet, and he smiles at her and nods when she asks him if he wants another Bass. He watches her as she goes to get them too, and I joke, "Not a bad lookin' dame, huh?"

"She's got big ones," he says grinning, so I cackle in appreciation like I'm one of his old buddies.

"She had big ones," he says again, so I cackle again.

"I felt her up," he says.

"You what? No, no, you didn't feel up the waitress," I tell him because now I'm afraid he'll say something to her.

"No, not her," he says, blinks and thinks about it. "In the cellar."

I nod but let it go. I have no idea what he's remembering or mixing up, don't feel like bothering to distract him. The serving wench brings our second round, and I watch to see if he looks at her big ones, not that she wouldn't be used to it with her serving wench cleavage designed for bigger tips. *She's sure got big tips*, I joke to myself. But he doesn't look at them. He's still thinking.

"She was crying." He looks down to his left and raises his arm a little like he can see her there, so the picture comes into my head too, her arms wrapped around his, her face buried in his shoulder. "It was dark, and it shook," he says, and I can't help asking, "Because a doodlebug exploded?" and he nods.

"Yeah. It was dark. We heard it buzz again. I was scared. It went quiet, and she was crying."

He doesn't tell me what's happening now, but his right arm moves underneath his left. His fingers curve and spread so it's clear what he's holding. He stays that way for a long minute, and I don't distract him. Why should I? What the hell's the harm? He's nineteen with one of her big ones in his hand. And who cares that it isn't Mom he's remembering? She was waiting for him with her smaller ones in Toronto, but what does it matter in the long run? In fact, my eyes start tearing up, and I want what he remembers, wish to hell it was mine. I've felt up, what, ten times as many women as he has? Twenty? But not like this, not so I'll remember it after so much else disappears like it never happened. The one you held for comfort when you thought a doodlebug would blow you up. Pretty soon he'd land at Juno and have a whole year of being scared without a breast to hold.

And then for no good reason except the random connection of Mom and breasts, I think of how I was premature, incubated for over a month, bottle-fed, bottle-fed afterward too. And I wonder for an instant if it explains something. People put so much emphasis on it now. Maybe I never bonded with her because I never touched Mom's breasts myself. But now I'm irritated and don't want to think of them because it feels perverted, pathetic too. Her breasts don't explain a thing. So I distract myself, drain my Bass and signal for another one, even though it means we'll be here longer because I won't drive drunk, *buzzed*, I think and scoff at the random connection with doodlebugs.

Dad stops feeling her up, raises his head and smiles.

"Nice round bum too," he says, so there's more to the story, but I don't want to go there, and it pisses me off a little that he says it. It's something else he's starting to forget, I'm noticing—how fathers and sons are supposed to talk to each other—more to the point, how they're not supposed to. But maybe that doesn't matter either in the long run, I think, and down my Bass.

He downs some of his with me like I've toasted him or maybe toasted her round bum. I gesture to the wench for another before I think about it, so when she turns to him and he nods, I say, "You sure that's a good idea?" Because all I want now is to sober him up, sober up myself, stop the buzz, I think with buzzed bitterness, get back in the truck. I'm afraid he'll pee himself now too, pee the truck seat, maybe even pee right here. I want to ask him if he needs to take a leak, but I look at the wench grinning at him, the grin he gives her back, and stop myself, spare him that small humiliation. She rolls her eyes toward me for the verdict though. She knows how to flirt with an old man and how to keep a younger one happy too who thinks he's in control. Younger, but not young, I think, because I'm an old man to her too, a lot creepier, in fact, if I look at her big ones. I respect her for it though, even if it is for tips. She's good. I shrug and nod, make a mental note to leave the kind of tip she wants.

"Hey, I gotta pee," I tell him. "How 'bout you?"

"Yeah," he says, so I help him up, walk at his elbow to make sure he's steady on the way. Then we stand side by side. He takes a little longer, so I ask if everything's ok down there. He turns his head with the kind of smirk I haven't seen in years.

"Swell," he says like I'm nuts. "Yours?"

So I laugh and feel better.

"Huge," I answer so he laughs too.

And when we get back to the table, I see that she's waited for us before drawing the beers so she can put them down and he can smile at her again. And this time he looks at her big ones, and she still takes her time, lets him, I think. And she doesn't say *You're cute* or wink, which is what young women say to old men smiling at them, but it reminds them they're old men too, and she seems to know it. You're good, I want to tell her, but it might break the spell, make her think I'm drunker than I am. She smiles at me too, though a lot more quickly, and I'm careful not to look at them.

He takes a swallow, looks glazed and happy, leans back in his armchair. "How's Annie?" he asks.

I let the question go, take a couple of swallows, say, "Do you remember the beer in England?"

"Yeah," he says, but that's all he says about it, and a second later he asks again like I didn't hear him. So I have to decide if I want to go back to straightening it all out, decide it doesn't matter enough to give him unpleasant details.

"She's fine," I say.

"She's a good girl," he says.

"Yeah."

"You should bring her with you. We can go out to dinner on me."

"Ok."

So he keeps his happy glaze, thinking about dinner with Annie.

"Does she still teach those kids with the problem?"

"Learning disabilities," I say.

"Yeah, does she still do that?"

"Yeah, she does."

"That's good. They need her," he says.

"Yeah," I say. "You're right."

So we both take sips of our beers thinking about Annie in our separate ways. What comes in my head is Annie in the dress with all the pockets, a crazy, gaudy, stupid dress left over from the sixties that we laughed at in a thrift shop in Santa Barbara. I count the pockets in my mind because suddenly it seems important to get it right. Four big ones around the waist, two more on the front, a smaller one on each sleeve and just below each shoulder, ten in all, hot pink and sunshine yellow on electric blue polyester. *Who needed cocktail dresses in the sixties?* I told her. *This one's perfect for acid parties. Just think of all the stuff that'd come out of the pockets.* We did for hours afterward sitting on the beach, all fun stuff at first. Disney cartoon birds and chipmunks, Snow White and all seven dwarfs, the mini-Beatles singing *Sergeant Pepper*, the entire cast of *Hair*. Later we did bad trips too. *Nixon*, I said. *Your mother*, she replied.

We bought it for the joke, but looking in the mirror at home, she said it really *was* perfect, and she was right. It became her

Friday dress. She filled the pockets with little rewards. *Like Pavlov's dog, huh?* I joked to tick her off. It did too, because she was sensitive about it, didn't like that kind of joke about her kids. And it really wasn't like that. She invited me to come one Friday and introduced me to them, one by one. One kid called me Mr. Pockets, got a laugh so that's who I was from then on. Skinny kid, blond hair, yellow teeth. Peter. Peter, Peter, processing problem. I helped Annie use her pockets, nothing like Pavlov. Everything cost something. *I have something for Peter in this pocket. What ever could it be? A hint costs the answers to only three questions.* And what came out of the pockets? Nothing much, just slips of paper half the time, *homework manager for the week*, a title for self-esteem, or some two-bit trinket, half a buck at most. Nothing and everything because she knew her kids, who they were, what each one wanted. That was the goddamned point of it, I'm thinking. The nothing, everything. I was the one with the processing problem. Does she still wear that dress? Probably, more than probably. I try to picture it, her hair gone gray but still in the Dorothy Hamill cut. Would she dye it? No, not her. Her face a little chubbier, her body making the damned thing look even more shapeless after a couple of kids. *Her kids.* I can hear her say it. He says something too.

"What?"

"What kids?"

"Well your ears still work pretty good," I tell him.

"Yeah," he says. "You said something about kids. I heard you."

"Oh, nothing, I was just thinking about something."

I look at his face and think of myself mumbling when I think too hard, wonder if he did it at my age. It's probably nothing, but then again, it's hard to know what's a sign and what isn't. Nothing, everything, I think. He looks worried now, sets his Bass down, chews his bottom lip. His eyes move.

"What's the matter? You feel ok? You sick to your stomach?" I'm thinking about him puking.

"No, I'm ok."

"What wrong then?"

"You have kids?" he asks.

"Oh, no," I say and reach across the chess table to pat his knee. "No, no kids. Don't worry, you didn't forget."

"Oh," he says, so I think about how strange it must be not to know that for sure. But he doesn't look that glad about not forgetting.

"What's wrong now?" I ask him.

"Are you going to?"

"Going to what?"

"Have kids," he says, "you and Annie."

"Oh, yeah," I say like I'm thinking it over. And then I do think it over, think what the hell?

"Why? Do you want grandkids that bad?" I ask.

"Yeah," he says and grins at it. So, what the hell, I think, give him one. Too late to take back what I said though because he might remember and be confused.

"Annie's pregnant," I tell him.

"What?"

"She's going to have a baby."

"She is?" he says so loud the serving wench looks up and then walks toward us. I try to shake my head to tell her we don't need her, but she's looking at him.

"Havin' fun?" she asks him, and he beams at her, doesn't care about her big ones now.

"Annie's having a baby," he tells her.

"She is?" she says beaming back.

"Yeah," he says.

She looks at me now, asks, "Your daughter?"

I just smile and let her think what she thinks. To say yes might confuse him, to say no confuse her.

"Well," she says, "that calls for a round on me."

"I don't think . . ." I start to say, but he drowns me out with his "Yeah," so she goes to fetch it. She walks around the bar to the kitchen first and comes out with a plate, looks happy as she draws the beers, a little smile on her face. That's all it takes for some women, I think, just the idea. She doesn't overdo it either, brings chips and miniature pasties with the beers, says, "On the house. Enjoy. Cheers and congrats." And she touches his shoulder with her fingertips as she walks away. She's good. I could fall in love with her, I think, think yeah yeah, feel old.

"Did you tell your mother?" he wants to know.

"Oh, uh, not yet, but I will," I tell him.

"Good," he says.

So we sit and munch the pasties and chips and drink the free beer. We don't say much more about Annie being pregnant, because we don't know what else to say. He eats and drinks intently, his head down. He's still got an appetite, still wolfs it fast, a habit he said he got in the army. He's happy, and it's good we have the distraction so I don't have to sit grinning or try to make conversation. I'm thinking about how women would go on and on about having a baby, but we don't know how to.

When he's done he leans back and smiles at me, buzzed and contented, and it's only a minute or two before he nods off. I let him. I'm buzzed myself, not ready to drive yet, and it's still quite a while before Happy Hour, so I don't try to wake him like Mom used to. Hold him to her standards. Which meant whatever happened to make her uncomfortable. She didn't like Annie either. Maybe I'm being unfair. Maybe because we never bonded, I think. Or maybe she had a processing problem. It makes me think of Annie pregnant again, the real one, not the one I made up. Her shy smile, happy and uncertain. *I thought we discussed this already. I thought we agreed.* Jesus Christ, I don't want to think about it, look around the room trying to think of England, anything. *I thought we discussed this already.* Hold her to your standards, whatever makes you uncomfortable. Maybe because you never bonded. Yeah, asshole, blame your mother, her little ones, too easy to do that. I look at him sleeping, wish I could remember it like I made it up for him. *My god, yes, I'm thrilled. It's scary but it's fantastic, beautiful. You're beautiful.*

Then I see the wet spot start to form, not much, just a few drops, a trickle, but it's happening. I get up and nudge his shoulder.

"Wake up, Dad. We should go," I say, lean over and whisper, "Come on, I'll take you to the head."

He's sleepy, confused. "I don't have to," he says.

"Yeah, you do. Come on."

I help him up, take his elbow again, and this time he's more staggery. On the way, I signal our wench for the check. She nods and smiles watching us, not a trace of pity in it. We stand side by side again, but he doesn't do much, a trickle, sways a little. "You ok?" I ask but this time he just says yeah and zips up, and we stagger out again.

Our wench doesn't offer any help, just sets the check down on the bar near us, mouths a thank you. She's perfect. Better not to offer help, less like it's a spectacle. I leave her most of my cash, nearly empty my wallet. What the hell do I need it for anyway?

I help him back into the truck, but I'm not ready yet, so we sit in the parking lot. He falls asleep again, of course, and I watch him for a while, wonder if he'll remember when he wakes up. Or maybe think he dreamed it. So I'm thinking of the Annie I made up, don't try to stop myself.

No, I'm thrilled. You're beautiful. We'll have to think what to name him. Or her. It doesn't matter. I don't care which. As long as it's ours. No, I know we agreed. But things are different now. I don't want you to do that. I don't. I changed my mind.

I think I smell pee and look, but he hasn't done anything. His eyes are open, glazed though as if he's still half dreaming. He blinks, and they clear a little, and he turns his head toward me.

"Are we going home?"

"Yeah, I'm waiting for my head to clear. I'll take you back in a little while."

"Will your mother be there?" he says, and I can see he isn't sure. I wish I could make something up, but I can't and then just take him back.

"No, Dad."

"Where is she?" he asks.

He's slumped sideways in the seat looking up at me, waiting. Like a kid, I think. I could tell him anything and he'd believe it, tell him she's gone to England if I want. He'd believe it, but that's not enough. He'd want to know when she was coming back, and I want to give him more.

"She's in heaven, Dad," I say.

His eyes move but slowly in his half-daze.

"There's no heaven," he says, because he's remembered that about himself, the self that didn't believe, that called religion a business, threatened to start his own.

Mom scolded and scolded him about it, but it didn't matter. *All it'd take is a big hat and a white suit, and the money'd roll in.* So I look at him and decide.

"No, Dad, there is. You're just mixed up. It must be the beer."

His eyes move a little more, but he asks what I expect him to.

"Are you sure?"

"Yeah, I am sure, and that's where Mom is."

He doesn't say all right, but I can see him thinking about it, making the right connections to believe it.

"What's it like?" he asks in a sleepy voice.

So I begin my bedtime story, Jolly Old Heaven, I think, the tourist version, nothing, everything.

"Well," I say, "it's like the best place you can think of, only better. And like the best feeling you ever had, only it never goes away. It never ends."

"It doesn't?"

"No, not ever."

"Oh."

From the collection of the Editor,
View from Wroxton Abbey, England, photograph

Andalucia

I can never get enough
of the juice that runs down my chin
from the peach I shared with my sister
one Saturday morning in July
when the sun cleared the steeple
and poured heat over us both
as if it had been pierced,
and the women shopping in the market
gobbled around us, and the sellers
hollered prices too fast to understand.
She wore my old white shirt
that was too small for her, the neck gapped open
and I felt embarrassed but didn't know why
when a blue-black strand of hair fallen like a wing
strayed down the front and the man with the rabbits in cages—
Dutch Lops—leaned forward to look
as she leaned down to look at them.
The lame boy with the crutch in the square
offered us his upturned palm
and she gave him our last peseta
but it didn't matter, we had enough, the peach
was so ripe the flesh was orange
and our hands were sticky
until we rinsed them in the fountain
and she took mine in hers
and said, "Here, let me"—
the water so cold it stung—
but her fingers warmed mine
and that fragrance in the sunlight
now always hers. "I don't want to go back,"
she said, "Not yet."

Heaven

Not that heaven does not exist, but that it exists without us.
—W. S. Merwin, "The Widow"

To begin with, they don't have wings.
That was just wishful thinking.
At night, they uncoil invisible ladders
and lower themselves, rung by rung.
"Something is missing," they think.
But they can't talk to one another here.
It has limits.
So they each begin the lonely inventory again.
They hear stones in a Mexican courtyard
crack and cool while the moon rises.
If bone gave light
it would look like this.
A dog barking somewhere
sounds like a man chopping wood
but there are no trees here.
Crows in the night
make a sound like a baby waking.
There must be trees.
There must be crows.
A child fallen into the well
while his mother is sleeping
finds the moon at the top of a stairway of water.
What is freely given
is freely taken away.

Vertigo

in memory of Czeslaw Milosz

The soul remembers that there is an up
and that there is down. It recognizes the earth
and the trees, the breadth of a Negev desert.

The soul knows the delicate, the livable layer
between dirt and the vast blank expanse
of the universe. The soul draws the horizon.

When my mother and I climbed the uneven steps
leading up one of Jerusalem's
narrow alleys, she made a mistake

and looked down. She became so dizzy
she had to sit, and ascend the remaining flight
on her hands and knees. Not one

of the passersby offered to help.
My mother said, *they think I'm climbing heaven's aerial stairs.*
On her hands and on her knees.

My soul stumbles
with the smallest of steps.
My soul knows only to keep moving.

In a big city, perhaps Paris or New York,
an émigré poet walks slowly
along foreign streets. In his arms, he carries
a microscope. Through it, the poet sees

that even on the tiniest scale *horror*
is the law of living things. The poet can't stop looking
through the eyepiece.

When my mother began to suffer vertigo,
my father and I simply pretended otherwise. One day
we rode glass-paned elevators. The next day,

it was huddled against the door. She said, *it's like crossing*
a suspension bridge in a hurricane.
She'd never been on a suspension bridge.

On bad days, my mother sat in her chair and barely
moved, never looking down or turning her head. The last month
of her life, she had trouble reading analog clocks.

The émigré poet writes poems about truth. People in exile
write many poems. He writes letters. In one, he asks the Pope, *what*
have they left to us?

My soul is vertiginous.
My soul shakes like dry sticks. My soul, trembling,
an atom flung loose.

Outside the window, a light wind blows
and hundreds of red and gold leaves rise up and up
over an ice-skinned river. This, though every tree I see

is bare. The leaves, defying even gravity,
from nowhere.

Explaining God to Israeli Children

Our existence is a ripple on the surface of God is not what Spinoza said but it's what he meant. And for making such heretic waves, Amsterdam's rabbis cursed him, expelling him from the Jewish fold in the same way, they said, Elisha condemned the jeering boys to the she-bear's paws and Joshua banned Jericho. The rabbis meant the Lord wouldn't spare him. Spinoza died ten years later gagging on invisible slivers of glass inhaled while grinding lenses. A death from a thousand cuts.

So When My Stepdaughter Asked About God, I Told Her

God's a lot like gravity. He pulls things
toward each other. Though sometimes he throws them
into space like a slingshot to be lost
forever. Then I told her, God's a means
of measure and like every number
has a unique place in a long list. And like God,

the numbers two and twelve don't exist
in space or time. But they exist.
A dozen eggs exist. Four hundred yards
of fabric. They'd exist even if we didn't
think of them that way. Pythagoras discovered
the height of sound is in inverse proportion

to the length of string plucked
to make that sound. He bowed down
before the number and thought it
absolutely divine. God is both an abstraction and
a real being, I said, the processor
of all things. She said, let's call him *Number One*.

It's not that I believe in an afterlife. When I die, I'll go back to the same place from which I was born. I imagine my body getting smaller and smaller, until the fetus devolves into the egg and sperm, then first the sperm, then the egg, wink out.

None of Pythagoras' writings
survive. Everything attributed to him
comes to us through others, just as to God.

My best friend believes God speaks with her in dreams and lis-
tens to her prayers. She asks me to pray for her or for things she
wants. God gave her diabetes and is slowly taking her eyesight.
Her older sister is planning for something more devastating. She
and her husband built a shelter and dug a well in the backyard of
their Connecticut mansion. They're installing their own electricity
generation equipment to be prepared for the pending Apocalypse.

I was maid of honor at my friend's wedding. In the basement of
the church where she married, there is a map showing the bibli-
cal borders of Israel. Israel, in this map, extends well into Jordan
and Syria, and even makes inroads into Egypt. My friend has never
tried to explain this map to me. This is how I know she loves me.

MESSAGE TO SPINOZA FROM ZBIGNIEW HERBERT:

> God wants to be loved
> by the paranoid and cursed
> because they hunger

Last week, my husband and I organized dinner for a business associate
of his visiting Israel from Utah. He's Mormon. The Mormon felt compelled to tell us that *his kind* identifies with Jews because they too were
persecuted. Later, when one of the Israelis told how his father helped
settle Jews in Israel during the country's first years, the Mormon said,
Your father must have been a Godly man. He was an atheist, the Israeli replied. *Here's to Jewish faith*, my atheist husband said, raising his glass.

MESSAGE FROM THE CHIEF RABBI OF ISRAEL WHEN ASKED TO LIFT SPINOZA'S
CURSE AFTER FOUR HUNDRED YEARS:

> There's no Spinoza
> and God only knows how much
> there's no Spinoza

Dark Night

at four score and eight
snow began falling
the world slowly changed
it went blank it grew strange
while wind kept insisting
december december
and blew out the cold tiny
stars one by one

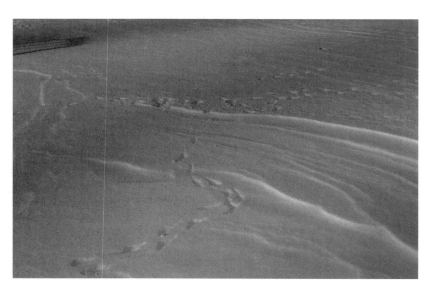

From the collection of the Managing Editor, photograph

C'est Freak

Ode to Stefan Bibrowski, aka Lionel the Lion-Faced Boy

*Lionel was discovered at the age of four by a German
showman known only as Sedlmayer, who took Lionel
and his mother to Berlin so the child could be exhibited.
While there, Lionel's mother abandoned him.*

Sedlmayer's was a life devoted to voyeurs of story
and spectacle. Handed a child, a disease, he created you
the legend: In 1890, Wilezagora, Poland, an escaped lion
eviscerated a man; his wife, sole witness to the beast,
beheld its face, forever imprinted on her unborn son. Given myth
and man, we indulge our desire to marvel: what of you is human,

what feral? What of the body beneath the bolero—the human
form beneath the fur? Feline echo of centaur, we amend the story:
add grace of line and limb, succumb to the nocturnal purr of myth,
each of our breaths is a whisper, a rumor of amber eyes that guide you
in the dark. We lap up each eerie drop: the insinuation of beast
beneath the starched and ruffled shirt, the mane of a lion

splayed across elegant shoulders and chest—regal as a lion,
a matador, a werewolf, a stunning mutation of human
genetic code; one in ten billion born changeling, born beast.
Foil to the beautiful cowardly king of the jungle, your story
summons violence, villagers, a hooded cloak, and escape. You
pounce upon our superstitions, beguile us with the music of myth,

our pleasure amplified by dusty accordion song, the myth
of The Lion Queen and Her Den of Untamable Lions;
by your gaze, as we imagine her attempts to tame you;
by Susi the Elephant Girl, Prince Randian the Human
Caterpillar. We kneel and extend our tongues to receive the story
wherein we imagine ourselves the opulent beast:

ours is the deadly paw, silent and lithe. We are beast
in body, spirit, or bed—players in the dark maze of myth.

We are mysterious, spectacular: muse and story
both, defined by repulsion and the insatiable desire to touch. A lion
makes magnificent the thirst to maim—a need our human
conscience denies, even as we savor our envy of you.

We hunger for the puncture and shearing of flesh; like you
would spurn the daily ritual, the methodical exorcism of beast
as we groom, pluck and preen. No longer in thrall to the hairless human
form, we revere the gods whose monstrous flaws make myth
and chosen men immortal. Without fur, Lionel the Lion-
Faced Boy would be nothing but an ordinary man—a story

none of us could entertain; nor is congenital hypertrichosis a story
to fascinate the world. It is the beast we want, the coat of a lion
usurping human skin, as thrilling as the punishments of myth.

from *Shadowed: Unheard Voices** *An Introduction and Speculations*

For over thirty years I have been in possession of a manila envelope crammed full of my great-aunt's fading photographs — her lingering artifacts, the last remaining evidence of her eighty-some years on earth. Their presence in my life instilled a nearly obsessive interest in the role that family photos, and especially snapshots, play in the formation and retention of personal memories. A precarious fortress against forgetting, photographs not only have the potential to help us remember, but they compel us to speculate. Undated and unnamed, the photos make me wonder: Who are these people and who were they to my Aunt Clo?

We have a multitude of perspectives from which to view old photographs: there is what we truly know, what we think we know, what we've misunderstood, and what we can only imagine. There is not only the photographed subject to consider, but the minor miracle of the photo's mere existence; the history of its long voyage before it landed in our laps, the many tears, creases, and stains acquired along the way — the inevitable fading. We contemplate the mystery also of an unknown photographer; a wide-brimmed shadow spread across silk dresses.

This breadth of speculation is the process into which we invited 27 poets. We collected and distributed a packet of 70 found photographs of women dating from the late 1800s to 1950. Each poet chose the images that most intrigued or inspired her, and then responded as poets do — with precision, color, texture, and rhythm. Collectively, we told our own truths. We speculated, we lied, and we dreamed, all in order to discover some kind of separate reality, a new truth behind the static images. Between the photographs and the poems, we let a dialogue emerge.

These are excerpts from a book about women and the photographs they left behind. It is about our truest and clearest memories, and the memories we make up. We've aspired to give a new life to the anonymous women in this collection, and to offer another dimension, another perspective from which to view our aunts and mothers and grandmothers. We've lifted the women in these photographs out of the shadows, if only to offer the briefest glimpse of who they might have been or who we wish them to be.

Shadowed: Unheard Voices edited by Joell Hallowell and Meg Withers

Because I am older now, I need a dog. I need tweedy clothes and a walking stick and a park bench on an autumn day. I need biscuits and tea and a hairnet, but most of all I need a dog. I need a dog that walks slowly and looks at me with certain eyes. I need a dog to feed twice a day, someone to groom. I need one with rheumy eyes and maybe a twitch or a limp. Here we are, the dog and I, limping toward you. A young man sees us and knows he has found the woman who should have been his mother. This is his mother before his eyes. This is his dog. He'll need to hurry to catch us.

malgrado ciò che puoi pensare nel vedermi sola
su questa piattaforma non sono ciò che tua madre (o la mia)
chiamerebbero una signora. Non mi manca la famiglia né
altro rumore — il chiacchierio vuoto come sassi
in una pentola di latta il suono della sua cravatta che scivola libera
nella nostra stanza da letto la sera. Ciò che volevo quando andai
era sedermi da qualche parte ad ascoltare il vento
sulle ali di uccelli quieti — il cra cra dei corvi
che ogni pomeriggio chiamano — i lenti sussurri del rosso
sangue che mi sale e scende in corpo.

Despite what you might think looking at me alone
on this platform I am not what your mother (or mine)
would call a lady. I do not miss my family or
other noise — the rattle of conversation like rocks
in a tin pan the sound of his tie sliding loose in our
evening bedroom. What I wanted when I left
was to sit somewhere and listen to the wind
in the pinions of settling birds — the gul gul gul of crows
that call each afternoon — the slow susurrus of red
blood rising and falling through my own body.

Tenía 17 años

Permanente recién hecho
     cortito
     vestido azul cielo

Iba a ser una dama de una novia en Santiago
     Amelia y yo

Fuimos a un estudio donde nos retrataron
     la primera vez que conocí una camara
     era el único lujo que teníamos

Ya tenía mis dineritos
     comencé a trabajar a los 16 años
     trabajabamos de servientas
     duré 4 años en esa casa

14 pesos por 3 o 6 retratos
     y uno los repartía
     "¡hay a mi prima!"
     "¡hay a mi tía!"
         era un lujo
         si me pedían, yo se los daba

I was 17 years old

Perm recently done
       short
       light blue dress

I was going to be a bridesmaid for a bride in Santiago
       Amelia and I

We went to a studio where they photographed us
       the first time I saw a camera
       it was the only luxury we had

By then I had my own money
       I started working at the age of 16
we worked as maids
I remained working 4 years in that house

14 pesos for 3 or 6 pictures
       one would give them out
       "this one for my cousin!"
       "this one for my aunt!"
           it was a luxury
           if they asked me for one, I would give it to them

Frank's eyes were a searing blue. Not ocean, not sky. Blue like white, like pictures of icecaps in strange cold places. There was a tree in front of her childhood home that looked like him. Climbing it, she'd scraped her knee. But in the dark against him she was cotton, she was flesh, she was water.

Turn away
Too much at stake in the looking
Your gloved hand upon my skirted thigh
Our buttoned chests.

I am trying not to hold
the past in my hand
to keep from jumping at the moon
or drinking from hollow cups
No one ever showed me how to do that trick
to cross my legs without lying still

The day Poppa died
he said, *Xie! Xie!* then collapsed
after thanking several hundred guests
at the end of his spring banquet speech
I ran to him and held him in my hands but
he had already gone

"Heck-la!" Mother ordered
rushing out of Sun Hung Heung after the ambulance
We couldn't stomach the *"gew yeung"*
nine courses of long life delicacies
piled in front of us as if covered with flies
"Mommy, what's the matter with *Goong-Goong?*"
my five-year-old asks stabbing at the empty bowl with her chopsticks

I remember the gentle warmth of his hand
like sunlight on a wound
I thought of the Buddhist nun, Junkyo Oisho,
whose hands were cut off at seventeen
by a jealous master who put his
five geishas to the sword as punishment
for his wife's infidelity
She learned to paint with her mouth
by holding the brush with her lips
"If the problem is a crippled body,
nothing can be done about it," she said
"But don't let your heart be crippled too!"

Light travels through space
just as memory through time
Thoughts fall in petals on my palm
When you weave your fingers through mine
What joy to behold the fullness of a hand
My heart cries, *Xie! Xie!*

Asher, I wanted America for her. Wanted life first. Education second. College and her own pocketbook. But even here she follows you, caring for every lost soul. Saving the drunks, the negroes, and now me. I tell her to go and she comes back with soup.

I pout because my upturned
brim has left my nose
exposed.
I can feel it redden—all
this hat for nothin'. Oh!
Cruel trick of millinery!

When my little snout is pink
as a suckling pig's, I know for sure
our swarthy companion will choose
my friend whose diving bell
of a chapeau has kept her lily-white
and supple as a peach.

He tips his face back to catch the sun
to be the dark and handsome one;

but I am ruddy
and undone.

Farm Kids

We were born to eat hotdish, to live in homes smelling
of hamburger or pork always, cigarettes sometimes. We were
towheads, most of us, in Kmart jeans and John Deere caps. We took

three trips a year to the big city, packed up the station
wagon with canned goods and pop to last for months. Our hands
grew strong from baling hay and carrying feed. We drank

at twelve or thirteen in our parents' car, somebody's
field, around a glowing fire in the gravel pits. The bar's neon
sign said *Drink Miller Lite*, so we did. We slept

through history, went to state with Future Homemakers
of America. The horizon seemed to end just a few miles
beyond our town near the flax field, a straight line

we crossed only for away games in the yellow bus. We mostly
went to church, mostly held on to our virginity after the dance
where the streamers waved like hands. We listened

to songs about getting out, identified with guitars and Tommy
and Gina, heard we weren't college material from the school
counselor but went anyway. We earned Masters and PhDs, moved

to places like Minneapolis or Anchorage where we learned
coffee grounds weren't always mixed with raw egg. We kept our eyes
forward. Most of us. A couple of us stayed: the teacher in training,

the undertaker's assistant, the farm kid who took the deed
and crawled into the dirty tractor cab, his eyes scanning the horizon,
his hands holding the wheel as if it would guide him there.

Genealogy

I can't keep them all straight
the one with the red beard the one
with the black the peasant girl in the
marketplace selling fruit and excitable Polish turkeys
who went to Toronto and who went to Cuba
who was a gymnast and who a soldier
who was incinerated and who saved even now
they come tumbling out of the womb the tips
of their fingers shaped exactly like thimbles ready to
baste to rip to alter to invisibly reweave

Todd Camp, *Broken Heart*,
acrylic, collage and encaustic on canvas, 12" x 12"

Cascade Plunge

On family Sundays our quarrels
were packed into one car, a Dodge
as old as I, and driven

for relief to a common water.
There, where no French suits or
unanointed feet were allowed,

we swam among the Baptists.
Daddy, under the filter-pump
water-fall, took the water as

I had not yet learned to,
letting it stream down his pate
in unnamed European rivers.

Mother sat out on the float,
forever gracious to farm boys
who climbed on only to belly-flop

off in a sweetheart's wake. And I
walked slowly around the pool, watching
the high-dive tower, where climbers,

some as young as I, would
jump. I could not believe
it was water they fell into —

rather some rare, personal fluid I had
not tasted, or would not with my
shallow plunges off the side

or the shoot-the-chute. And whether
it was fear or not that kept me
from my falls, I do not remember

or care, having fallen since,
older, deep and unfathered
into other waters.

Barbara A. Fischer

Prodigals

Dad's coffee cup trembles in his hands. "Not for me," he says in a pained voice when Mother tries to put a spatula of scrambled eggs on his plate. It's been four days since he's had a drink. My older sister Reenie and I don't bicker and jostle for leg room under the table. Mother slips quietly into her chair, and like Reenie and me, focuses on her own plate. Yet we're all aware of Dad's eyes darting restlessly to the counter where the Harvey's Bristol Cream props up the cookbooks. Dad gets up. The cookbooks slip sideways as he lifts the bottle. Back at the table, he pours a generous splash into his cup, then lifts it up as if to say, *to us.*

Reenie and I relax. Dad is back. Now we can go back to being who we really are. Reenie can be her goody-two-shoes self and I can be Dad's feisty little show-off. Mother smiles at Dad, but just slightly. Her just-slightly smile is her most beguiling, a complicated mix of disappointment, commiseration, and relief, which adds up to something like comfort. Not approval, exactly. More like acceptance, as if our flaws and weaknesses are dear to her because they're ours. Who could blame Dad for choosing Mother over the cold mean people who raised him?

Dad was forever telling us stories about life with those people of his. The long hungry hours before dawn carrying water to the horses, the icy afternoons repairing barbed-wire fences, the dark evenings listening to his father read from Scripture while the wind whistled down the cold chimney. "We didn't have summer back then," he always said.

Reenie and I thrilled to his stories. They were like fairy-tales, funny and horrifying, comic and cruel. We weren't fooled by the sunny way he told them. Like fairy-tales, we knew they were about dark, terrible truths.

"Let me tell you a little story about work ethic," Dad says several weeks later when Mother complains that Reenie and I have failed to make our bed again. He's just come home from work and hasn't even had his first drink yet.

"My old man spent fourteen hours a day digging rocks out of a frozen field," he says sternly. "But no matter how much he wanted to melt his beard by the fire, if one of us boys left a chore undone, bone weary as he was, back out in the cold he went to whup us good behind the barn with the cat o'nine tails. *He* wasn't afraid of a little work. Mercedes!" he shouts to Mother. "What'd you do with the cat o'nine tails?" Then he squints out the kitchen window to the alley behind our rowhouse in Philadelphia and asks, "And what'd you do with the barn?" Mother sighs and smiles, just slightly.

That night at dinner Reenie flattens her mashed potatoes and deconstructs her meatloaf but doesn't take one bite. After dinner we move to the living room to watch Rowan and Martin's *Laugh-In* with our Mrs. Smith's cherry pie wedges balanced on plates on our laps. Reenie doesn't touch hers, even though cherry pie is her favorite. I know what she's doing. She's punishing herself for not making the bed. Going to bed hungry was the standard punishment for any minor wrongdoing when Dad was young.

"Watching your girlish figure?" Dad asks Reenie. A joke. Reenie, at eleven, is skinny as a razor. Reenie doesn't laugh. Reenie rarely laughs at anything, least of all at herself. Other people are always doing that for her. At school they call her Bagga Bones.

"When I was young," says Dad, drink in hand, "all we had for supper was boiled okra and we licked our plates clean. Wasting food was a terrible sin. Imagine what a sin it would be to waste cherry pie. Not that we knew such a thing as cherry pie existed. I didn't know what sugar was until I met your mother. Isn't that right, Mother?"

"Call me Mother again and you'll never get sugar in this house either," she says.

My parents exchange a private smile. Dad drapes one arm around Mother's shoulders and pulls her close. He extends his other arm to Reenie and me. I go to snuggle with them on the sofa. Reenie doesn't. She never does. Instead she watches us with a mixture of envy and dislike, the same way I imagine Dad's people would if they could see us laughing and tangled together on the sofa. They're who we're showing off for. That's why we need Reenie. We need her disapproval to remind us how happy we are without it. And maybe to protect us against it, as if Reenie carries some benign form of a disease that works like a vaccine to keep us all safe from a nastier, full-blown case.

It doesn't always work.

It's close to ten o'clock on a Sunday morning. Reenie and I are playing jacks on the linoleum at the bottom of the stairs when

Dad comes down. He's in his robe, barefoot, his face a mask of black stubble. Mother, also in her robe, her hair standing up in lacquered points, has been up for about ten minutes. She's gathering saucers of cigarette butts and harvesting crumpled napkins. They had one of their parties the night before. Reenie and I were used to sleeping through them. Dad steps on a jack and lets loose a string of wondrous curse words.

"Cover your lily-white ears, girls," Mother laughs.

Dad doesn't laugh. He says, "Let me tell you a little story." He sounds cranky. He usually does on Sunday mornings.

"If your Grandfather Joachim could see you wasting precious time on a little bouncy ball and twisty pieces of metal," he says, "he'd send you to the root cellar to keep the turnips company. Make you stand there all day in the dark with nothing to do. Try that for ten hours and you'd have a different opinion of idleness, I guarantee it."

I knew that most of Dad's stories were exaggerated way past the point of truth. I didn't really believe that he and his brothers had to take turns eating because they only had one fork or that they only got to wear one sock each because there weren't enough pairs to go around. But spending an entire day in the root cellar? That strikes me as true.

Mother's on her way to the kitchen holding five glasses in her hand, a finger deep into each like a glass claw. Dad pulls the glass from her thumb, and the others, each depending on the next for balance, slide off her fingers and bounce on the carpet. "Jimmy," Mother complains, more weary than irritated. She drops the balled-up napkins and steps on them in her fuzzy slippers to sop up the spills. Dad sinks into the sofa and swallows the inch of liquid in the glass he's pulled from Mother's hand.

"What're you all staring at?" he snaps. "Pay no attention to the grouch on the sofa. Who is he to judge?" He reaches for a lipstick-stained glass from the end table and swallows what's left in that. "Quit *staring* at me," he says. "Just . . . go on. Go on and play."

Reenie and I don't move.

"I said play!" Dad thunders. "*Play!*"

I try to hand the ball to Reenie but she won't take it.

"Jimmy," Mother says with pointed gentleness.

111

Dad runs his hands over his face and scrapes them up through his hair. When he uncovers his face, he's wearing a completely different expression. The deep frown is gone. He's smiling—or trying to. But Reenie and I, being children, recognize the look of someone who's trying hard not to cry. We know this look. We've seen it before. During birthday parties. On Christmas mornings. We know we're not responsible for his rare, ugly rants against us. But the sad, beaten look that comes over him afterwards? We are responsible for that.

❊ ❊ ❊

I never thought of my father's parents as my grandparents. We never saw them. They lived far away in farm country, another world. Yet they took up more room in our lives than Grandma and Grandpa Webb, my mother's parents, whom we saw several times a week. When Dad was his normal happy self, I almost forgot about those parents of his. But when he came down with one of his moods, I could feel them in the room with us. Then I'd realize that they never went away. And that it wasn't Dad's fault, or ours, that happy things made him sad. It was his parents' fault. They didn't believe in happiness. They didn't want him to be happy.

Yet Dad still went to see them. It defied logic, like the cheerful way he told his stories about them. He'd even taken Reenie and me to visit them once when we were very little, without Mother, when I was about four and Reenie about six.

"Your Grandmother Joachim was just tickled with you, Chloe," Dad says to me in one of his fond remembering moods. "My little apple-cheeked girl, she called you."

Mother and Dad are drinking Manhattans on the teeny patio in front of our house on Renwick Street. Reenie and I are sitting on the stoop eating cherry Popsicles. All the neighbors are out. It's too hot to be inside. The sun is a smoldering red ball sinking into purple clouds.

"Did Grandmother Joachim like me?" asks Reenie.

"Well of course she did," says Dad. "But Chloe was still small enough to be rocked in her lap. You took right to your Grandmother Joachim, Chloe. Remember? Remember your Grandmother Joachim rocking you?"

"No," I say, though I wished I could say yes and that I'd hated every minute of it. I was sure I had. But really, I couldn't remember.

"I remember," says Reenie. "I remember Grandmother Joachim's. Her kitchen sink had a pump handle where the faucets should be. She tied an apron around my neck and moved a chair over so I could work it."

"I don't know how you talked me into letting you take the girls to that place, little as they were," says Mother. "I worried all day that someone would try to baptize them in the river."

"River was frozen," says Dad. "Mother wouldn't have turned Chloe loose long enough, anyway. She sat and rocked her all afternoon. Probably the longest Mother sat down in her whole life." To Reenie and me he says, "She never had any little girl babies of her own. Just us trouble-making boys."

"Boys kept coming in and going out," says Reenie. "Noisy boys. Or maybe," she stops, remembering, "maybe just the same boy. Grandmother Joachim kept saying, 'In or out!'—just like Mother."

"My brother Joseph's boy," says Dad. "Your cousin. They lived there for a time after their house burned."

"The boy wanted to go ice skating," says Reenie. "But Grandmother Joachim kept saying no. Remember? But then you talked her into it. I wanted to go skating with you and the boy too but you wouldn't let me. I had to stay in the kitchen. I think I started to cry. I think that's when Grandmother Joachim let me play in the sink."

"You *left* them?" says Mother. "You left them *alone* in that house?"

"Not alone. With my mother. You have to understand, Mercedes. You don't let a perfectly good frozen-over pond go to waste."

"Grandmother Joachim kept telling you to listen for the ice," says Reenie. "She said it had a song."

"What your Grandmother Joachim meant," says Dad, "was to listen for the special sound the ice makes when it's in danger of cracking. It's a kind of singing sound. Like when you hit a saw with a hammer. Bet you city girls have no idea what you do when you hear that singing sound when you're way out on the ice."

"Head for shore quick," I guess.

"Nope. You move away from the people you're skating with, to lessen the weight," says Dad. "Hard to do if you're skating with your sweetheart. Yes, I admit it. I knew what a sweetheart was before I met your mother."

"What was her name?" asks Mother. "Don't tell me you don't remember." She's only pretending to be angry now.

"Rebecca," says Dad. "Big strong country girl. Never once thanked me, nor forgave me, for shaking her off and skating away from her."

"I wouldn't either," says Mother.

"They'd have had to dredge the pond for our bodies," Dad says to Mother, "if you'd been my sweetheart then."

❊ ❊ ❊

When I was ten, Dad's father was run over and killed by his own tractor. We got the call on a Sunday night when we were eating Pepperidge Farm layer cake and watching the Smothers Brothers. Dad's father had bled to death two hours before. I don't know who made the call—his people didn't believe in phones. All I remember is Dad saying, "It can't be. It's *Sunday*," like he thought he could convince the person on the other end that there'd been some mistake.

"But it's Sunday," Dad kept repeating after he hung up. "Someone's got it wrong. It can't be. It's *Sunday*."

"Sunday's the Sabbath," Reenie whispers to me. "They're not supposed to operate machinery on the Sabbath. They're not supposed to work at all." I don't know how she knew such things, she just did.

My parents had a long, drawn-out fight about going to Grandfather Joachim's funeral.

"Wouldn't it be better if you took the girls without me?" Mother asks. "You know they don't want me there."

"I want you there," Dad says.

"But think of them. The last thing they need at such a difficult time is someone they disapprove of, right there in their church, when they'd rather be thinking only good holy thoughts."

"See what she's doing?" Reenie, twelve, whispers to me as we eavesdrop from the top of the stairs. "She's trying to make it sound like *she's* the one thinking the good holy thoughts. Really, she just doesn't want to go."

"Neither do I," I say. "Do you?" I'm on Mother's side. I usually am. This doesn't stop Dad from liking me best.

"Well, no," Reenie says. I don't believe her. Reenie, I suspect, thinks of the Joachims as the family she should have had, the family that would see beneath her dull dreary plainness to discover . . . even more dull dreary plainness, which would look like virtue to them. "But it is our duty," she adds.

"They don't disapprove of you," we hear Dad say. "They don't know you, is all. They're fearful of what they don't know."

"They don't *want* to know me," says Mother. "They've made that crystal clear. But I don't want to get into all that right now. Let's just say I don't want to make a hard day any harder for them. Let's just leave it at that."

They don't just leave it at that. Reenie and I don't have to hide to listen. We can hear them shouting at each other in their bedroom half the night.

"These are people who refused to come to our wedding!" we hear Mother say.

"You know it's against their beliefs to attend services in another church," says Dad. "They're simple people. All they have are their beliefs. You might try being less judgmental about other people's beliefs."

"Judgmental? *Judgmental?* They judged *me*, sight unseen. Are you not dead to them for marrying me?"

Actually, Dad was only dead to his father—which we knew from Grandpa and Grandma Webb, who must have heard it from Mother. Dad's mother always welcomed him home, but Dad's father refused to see him whenever Dad visited.

"If you'd *let* them get to know you," says Dad, "if just once you got off your high horse and went to see them like I've been begging you to for years, all might be forgiven. But no. Oh no. Not you."

"*Forgiven?* For what? For marrying you or for being who I am? Why would you want them to forgive me for *either*?"

When it came to arguing Dad was no match for Mother, yet he trumped her every time. All he had to do was run a helpless hand through his hair and say—or only think—*I need you. I need you to be on my side.* Their fights always ended with Mother's crooked little half-smile of graceful surrender. With conditions.

❊ ❊ ❊

"If I do go," says Mother.

It's the night before the funeral. We're at the table. Mother has heated up the enormous pot of lamb stew Grandma Webb brought over when she heard about Dad's father. Apparently that's what people did when there was a death in the family—they delivered food no one wanted to eat. Dad stares into his bowl as if he can't figure out what it's for. He looks up. Reenie and I do, too. We all heard Mother say *if*. A word of surrender if ever there was one.

"If I do go," Mother says, "I'm going as myself."

Dad nods cautiously.

"I'll be quiet and respectful. I won't cause a scene. But I *will* be the woman you married anyway, against their wishes. *If* I go."

"That's all I ask," says Dad. "The woman I married, at my side."

"Plus you need me to drive," says Mother, reaching out to steady his shaky hands. He's on the wagon again, in preparation for his trip home.

"I need you," Dad agrees.

The next morning Mother tells Reenie and me to put on church clothes. I assume she means what we wear when Grandma and Grandpa Webb take us to Mass on Easter Sunday—frilly pastel dresses and lacy anklet socks. Reenie tells me those clothes won't do—not at this church. In olden times, she says, Dad's people scratched their cheeks and tore their garments when someone died. Nowadays, she says, things were more relaxed, but you still had to look like you were so filled up with loss that you didn't care what you looked like. She gives me one of her sack-like jumpers to wear. She has a closet full of them. What loss, I wonder, is Reenie mourning?

My patent leather Mary Janes would be disrespectful, Reenie says. She digs deep in our closet for a pair of the corrective shoes she's outgrown. Reenie is bowlegged. When she stands with her feet together her knees remain five inches apart. She has to wear shoes you need a prescription for, like glasses. They make her feet—and now mine—look like submarines.

Mother is wearing a little black dress that comes just to the middle of her knees. It has a form-fitting jacket with a sparkly oversized button at its tight cinched waist. Despite the fact that it's black, there's nothing mournful about her outfit. Reenie in her shapeless gray jumper and clumsy lace-up shoes looks like a nun by comparison. And so, I realize, do I.

Dad is standing behind Mother at the mirror over the bureau in their bedroom as she squirts her bouffant with hairspray. "That's what you're wearing?" he asks. We know he isn't talking to Reenie and me.

"Meaning?" says Mother.

Reenie and I exchange glances. If this is a test — and of course it is — Dad is flunking.

"Just that . . . " Dad hedges. "You know how these people of mine are."

Normally Dad referred to them as *those* people, like they were a strange tribe with weird customs. But *these* people? Of *mine?* Again, I'm on Mother's side. I want to be on Dad's. He's my favorite parent. But we are his family and he needs to choose us.

"All I'm saying," says Dad. "Well, that lipstick, for instance. Isn't it a bit . . . festive? Don't you have anything less . . ."

"Less me? Nope." Mother applies another layer of Persian Melon to her lips. "Girls," she says, "what do you think of this shade?"

"It's beautiful," I say. And so is my mother.

"Want some?" she says to me. "Come here, then. Purse your lips." She coats my lips, hands me a tissue, and says, "Blot." I know exactly what to do. I've watched her countless times before this very mirror, envying her beauty, her cosmetics, her toys. I bite the tissue and look at myself. It's like magic. My mother's lips, full and pouty, on my own face. I look like my mother. I'd never realized. *This is why Dad loves me*, I think.

"Reenie?" says Mother, holding out the lipstick. "You could do with a little color. Come here, honey."

"I will *not*," says Reenie. It's almost a hiss. She's never spoken in such a tone before.

Mother shrugs, recaps her lipstick and drops it with a clink into her beaded clutch purse. Dad runs both hands through his hair. He knows when he's beat.

❊ ❊ ❊

Dad's people lived far away in farm country in a place I always thought of as the great unknowable beyond. Yet as we travel the twisty roads beyond the congested city, I recognize certain landmarks—the silo with the silver star, the enormous stone house with the six leaning chimneys, the little grocery store painted shocking pink, the gas station with the old-fashioned pumps. I've been on these roads before. During our Sunday afternoon drives.

Sunday afternoon drives were our version of church. About six times a year after one of Mother and Dad's long Sunday afternoon naps, which always took place after one of Dad's ugly rants, we'd go driving. Most recently, two weeks before.

"Beautiful country," Dad had said. He'd sounded calm and relaxed. He always did after a long nap with Mother. "Admit it, Mercedes," he'd said. "It's appealing, isn't it? Blessed peace and quiet. No noisy neighbors."

"*We're* the noisy neighbors," Mother said.

"You girls could have pets if we lived in the country," Dad said to Reenie and me. "You could have your very own cow. Imagine having your very own cow to milk. Wouldn't that be fun?"

"I'd just as soon walk to the Kwik Mart for a quart," I said from the back seat.

"Reenie, you'd milk the cow for your old man, wouldn't you, so he'd have fresh cream for his coffee?"

"I guess," said Reenie.

"That's my girl!"

I watched the thoughts turn in Reenie's head. I saw her thinking how different things would be if we lived on a farm like the Joachims. There, she'd get to be my father's feisty little show-off while I'd be the sullen child who watched with envy.

Now, on our way to the funeral, we go farther than we ever went on our Sunday drives. We bump over potholed roads that get smaller and smaller. We pass leaning shacks with caved-in porches, weedy yards full of rusty car parts, cows knee-deep in mud with tails matted to their hindquarters. The country, apparently, had its own version of the slums. Mother is driving.

"Turn here," says Dad. "And pull over." Mother stops but doesn't pull over. The road is too narrow.

Dad takes his silver flask from the glove compartment, twists it open, takes a few long swallows then offers it to Mother. Mother shakes her head then changes her mind. They open their car doors and get out to switch places. I don't need Reenie to tell me it wouldn't do for Dad's people to see Mother behind the wheel.

Reenie digs into her jumper pocket and pulls out two sticky candy canes left over from last Christmas. She breaks each in half and offers us all a piece.

"Thank you, my dear," says Dad. Mother says nothing as she crunches down on hers. I stare at the half Reenie's handed me. It's furry with lint. The red stripes have bled pink onto the white. "We all need to smell the same," she whispers to me. "They'll notice if only *they* smell like peppermint."

Dad can't seem to get the hang of the clutch. We lurch and jerk along a dirt road—more of a path, really, until we arrive at a small cinder-block building with long, narrow windows. I wouldn't have known it was a church if it hadn't been for the steeple and the cemetery behind. Mud-splattered pickups and junky dented cars are parked at all angles. We get out. Mother's high heels punch precise little holes in the dirt as we walk to the church.

Inside it's chillier than outside. There aren't any pews. People sit on folding chairs or stand against the walls. A boy of about fifteen with a cold sore on his lower lip meets us inside the door. He and Dad clasp hands then hug each other hard. The boy leads us to the front where empty chairs are waiting. Mother's heels go clickety-click on the linoleum. Everyone watches us but pretends they're not. I watch them the same way.

All the men have beards and are dressed in clean, pressed suits shiny with age. The women have long, flowing hair—beautiful hair, which I envy since Mother makes Reenie and me keep ours short and permed. The women are not all wearing sack-like dresses like Reenie and me. Their clothes are worn-looking, too, but like the men, they've obviously gone to some trouble with their appearance. I see strings of pearls, glints of gold in earlobes. And Mother is not the only woman wearing lipstick and face powder. But she is the most stylishly dressed. For the first time in my life, I'm a little ashamed of Mother. It's not polite, the way her brand-new clothes make theirs seem so shabby and old-fashioned.

The preacher comes out from behind a curtain and stands behind a podium set on a card table. He's thin, shaggy, and, like Dad, a little shaky. There's a great clattering of chair legs against linoleum as everyone stands. The preacher reads from the Bible, his Adam's apple bobbing with every word. He doesn't look up as he reads, doesn't seem particularly moved by his words. It's like being at a PTA meeting in the gym listening to Mother read the minutes from the last meeting. The readings go on and on.

Then the preacher closes his Bible and fixes us with a look that feels like lightning.

"Pray for God's mercy!" he booms. I'd never have guessed he had such a voice in him. So much time goes by that I think that's all he's going to say.

Then he says, "Why, Lord? Why take John? A good man, a good provider, a hard worker who served You faithfully, unfailingly, all the days of his life. Who among us has not asked ourselves this today?"

Around me I see heads drop in silent admission.

"Pray for God's mercy," the preacher roars, "those who question His will!"

Another long silence.

"Lord, You have told us to keep holy the Sabbath. Brother John failed to obey Your Word. And so You cut him down. Who among us has not thought this today?"

People clear their throats and shuffle their feet.

"Pray for God's mercy," the preacher shouts, "those who sit in judgment!"

When he speaks again, his voice is a whisper. Everyone leans forward to hear.

"We are forgiven," he says. "Those who doubt. Those who sit in judgment. Those who challenge God's will. Even those who dare to stand before you and interpret His word. Yes, even I am forgiven."

He leans forward with his elbows on the podium. "Dear people," he says. Now he sounds like he's talking to friends. "We are created in God's image. Yet in our imperfect understanding, in our confusion, we think it's the other way around. We think God must be like *us*. We put ourselves in God's place. We tell ourselves, 'This is how God feels.' Forgive me. Forgive me now as I do the same.

"Because now I imagine God looking down on John plowing his field. I imagine God thinking, with great love, 'He is working my fields. He toils to gather the harvest I have provided lest any should be wasted.' Imagine with me now God's sorrow as He takes John from his work. From us. For reasons none of us can comprehend.

"Yet we try to comprehend. We try to find reasons. It's because he was working on the Lord's Day, we say to ourselves. It's because John didn't trust You, Lord, to provide another day in which to finish His work.

"Dear people. I believe that God *did* feel sorrow that John did not keep holy His day. But John's disobedience hurt John most of all. God's word lights our path. Disobedience dims that light. Without the light, we stumble and fall. That's why God hates sin so, dear people. Sin is that which hurts *us*.

"Think of your love for your children. Think of your anger when they disobey and put themselves in harm's way. Do you wish them greater harm, greater hurt, for their disobedience? No. You'd gladly bear your children's pain, if you could. As our Savior did for us, on the cross. You weep when your children stumble and fall. As Jesus wept. As Scripture tells us: *Jesus wept*. But think how you'd rejoice if your children's pain was yours to bear!

"People. On this sorrowful day, God leads us to an even greater understanding of Him. Today, He invites us to join Him. As He weeps. As He forgives. As He rejoices. For John *is* with God in Heaven today. And no hurt will come to him there! What a great gift we have been given today. To be like God Himself. To weep, to forgive, and then to rejoice."

Dad and Reenie can't get past the weeping part. Their shoulders pulse with sobs. Mother, dry-eyed, passes Dad and Reenie a steady stream of Kleenex from her beaded purse.

❖ ❖ ❖

It's cold in the cemetery in back of the church. An icy wind blows. When we left home it was October, the sky a deep cloudless blue. Here, it feels like winter. Maybe Dad wasn't kidding, I think, when he said they didn't have summer.

In the short walk from the church to the cemetery I get separated from Mother, Dad and Reenie. At first I can see them ahead of me but then the backs of strangers interrupt. Gradually I become aware of an old woman walking beside me. My grandmother. In church she'd been surrounded by men—her sons—and I hadn't been able to get a good look at her, but now, somehow, I know her. And can almost remember the tick of her heart as I lay curled against her in the rocking chair.

At the grave site, she places her hand on my chin and turns my face to hers. She isn't much taller than me. Her skin is loosely draped over the bones of her face, puddling in wiggly folds under her chin. Her cheeks are pebbled with little black moles like raised freckles. She reaches into her coat pocket—a man's coat—and pulls out a thin yellowed hanky, spits on it, and wipes the lipstick off my mouth.

"I'm not blaming you, child," she says as she scrubs. "Don't think that. I know. We all want a bit of pretty sometimes. Believe me, I know." The cold air stings the wet places on my mouth.

"But we need to make do with what we're given," she says, "and be grateful for it." She inspects my face then releases her grip on my jaw. "Hard not to want more, though, isn't it?"

She doesn't seem to be talking to me anymore. For a moment, she reminds me of Mother and Dad when they exchange their private looks.

"It's pretty here in the spring," she says. "Wild roses. Lilacs. Peony bush comes up right over there. And that crabapple tree over the Schmidts' stone? Full of crazy blossoms every May. No sign of none of that now, though, and just as well, I suppose. All that plenty would just make it harder, wouldn't it? You see how plain can be its own blessing."

She drapes her arm across my shoulder and pulls me to her side. I see Mother and Dad on the other side of the circle standing in a tight knot of men and women. The men are gathered on either side of Dad. They must be my father's brothers. I can see the resemblance despite their beards. The women, their wives I suppose, make their own little group on either side of Mother. One of the wives looks younger and less raw-boned than the others. She and Mother lean into each other, smiling and talking discreetly, the young wife reverently touching the beads on Mother's clutch purse.

And then I see Reenie. She's standing several paces to the left of Mother and Dad. There must have been other people around her, but now I recall a solitary figure huddling into herself. And though I know her dress comes down to her calves, I sense the space between her knees and can almost feel the chilly air between them. She must feel me looking at her because she defiantly pulls herself up and regards me not with bitterness but with something like it, a cold acceptance, her eyes on Grandmother Joachim's hand resting lightly, warmly, on my shoulder.

D.C. in '69

It's August in Montrose Park.
Nixon is in the White House.
Jowly, sweaty babies
discover how to creep
up the metal slide.
Heads down, slapping
sticky hands, they rise.

Everywhere the scent
of patchouli,
a slight scratch in the eyes
of tear gas and pollen,
osage orange
plasters the playground.
The intrepid babies move
through it all
to retake the slide.

A flute plays at a picnic,
yellow-jackets drop
down to the cherries,
probe the red flesh,
helicopter out.
This is the fourth week
of tropical heat.
Riots are expected.
Families pour ice water
over their mattresses
on sleeping porches
across the city.

We watch the four-year-olds,
swinging, swinging
as if they could catapult
over the fence,
down Rock Creek Parkway
on the strength
of their skinny arms
their tough pumping legs,
oblivious
to all but the rush
of the slight breeze
they've generated,
heads thrown back,
taking big gulps
out of the bleached air.

Glenn Herbert Davis, photograph

Funereal

The women here wrap their dresses under their shins.
Their voices leave the meetinghouse for the tree-beds
and the cracked sheet-metal roofs. Plumerias cover
the floor where a basket of money sits, where my father
shakes hands. Braided fronds loosen on the fence
by the road, and girls who knew my brother well
crouch by the wall looking in. Their hands are red
from plucking the rusted wire of a window.
I'm watching my mother fan the face and touch
the mouth with oil. I'm watching my cousins
who wear collared shirts pass a bag of betelnut
between them. My oldest uncle leans on a pipe
with his arms bulging from his sleeves. The generator
clicks in, and shadows fade from the unpounded nails,
from the sagging beams. I'm told they found him
two compounds from here, by the dying breadfruit tree,
by the house of a girl he went with, a spot he swept
the leaves from. In the waiting line aunties ask for plates,
for the one bin of pig meat. They ask if I've had enough.
I remember shoving him to the edge of his truck
in front of my father and kicking a bruise into his knee.
I remember he slashed a V into my arm and ran off
to carve his canoe. And on the tables, flies pull bits
of fish from the bones left by men I'm told are uncles.
I've never met them. Men file through with bags of rice.
Boys sit by the door or wait in the picked-apart cars
where tapioca grows from the engine or up the coiled
metal under the seats, where even the floor is rotted out
and blooming.

Collage Poem

This little mole has been working
very hard all morning spring cleaning
her little house while on the sea once
upon a time o my best beloved there
was a whale and he ate fishes a way
a lone a last a loved a long the river-
run past Eve and Adam's where
all happy families are alike as they dance
by the light of the moon but how
can we know the dancer from the dance
unless we are Marie of Roumania and all
that mumbo jumbo will hoo-doo you
until you go home and get kicked
downstairs or put a bullet through
your head . . . shantih shantih shantih

From the collection of the Managing Editor, photograph

The Pygmy Queen

Morning, October. The family is having breakfast by the swimming pool, where the light casts marbled patterns in the glowing water. An umbrella covers most of their table in shade, but Glenda, the grandmother, sits in a wedge of sun. She is looking up at two storks perched on the pool-house roof. They are tall, hunchbacked birds, with black eyes and beaks that hang like scowls. They probably disapprove of the family's choice of breakfast foods, the soy sausages and slice-and-bake rolls. They've come seeking carrion, fish straight from the sea.

At the table with Glenda sit Paul, her son, and Anna, her teenaged granddaughter. Neither has noticed the birds. Paul is walled in by an unfolded newspaper, and Anna is asleep, her head against the stone tabletop. Beside her is a plate of untouched food.

They are waiting for Val, Paul's wife, who is inside, dawdling with the coffee. She has a gift for turning the simplest tasks into long, involved endeavors. Glenda is in no hurry, but Paul has to leave for the office and Anna for school. Val hasn't found a practice to join since the family moved to Florida, so she works from home, seeing her few patients in the cottage that Glenda and Dwight used for overnight guests.

Anna's lips twitch; she is dreaming. Glenda doesn't know how she can sleep like that, with her head against the stone. She reaches out and touches the girl's blond head. Anna's eyelids flutter, but they do not open.

"Okay," says Val, sliding open the deck door. "Here it is." She is holding her French press, which she insists on using even though Glenda owns a coffee machine. Val is a particular woman, in many ways the opposite of Paul, who doesn't notice where his coffee comes from or who makes it, as long as he has a cup before heading out the door. He has changed little in the twenty-five years since he last lived under Glenda's roof. In the morning, he is still quiet and rumpled, with his cheeks creased in pillowcase lines. His hair still grows in the same funny way, straight up from his fore-head, but where he used to comb it down with gel, he now uses only water.

"Look," Glenda says, once Val has arrived at the table. She points up at the storks. "Those sour-pusses think they're going to have some of our breakfast. But they won't find what they're looking for here!" She calls up to the birds: "My granddaughter's a vegetarian!"

Anna lifts her head, her cheek indented by the pores of the stone. Paul lowers his newspaper, and Val puts a hand over her lipsticked mouth. "Paul," she says. "Those are vultures."

Glenda starts to correct her, but her voice is lost under the sound of Paul's throat-clearing. Poor Paul has a good deal of phlegm; he is allergic to three-quarters of the year in Florida. Glenda waits to hear what he will say. She doesn't like to interrupt him, especially when he has to work to clear his airways.

"Well, that's unacceptable," he musters. He lays his newspa-per over the table so that it covers his daughter's plate, and before Glenda can say a word, is up and striding toward the pool-house, the door of which he swings open so hard it hits the outside wall. He disappears inside, doubtlessly looking for a long stick of some kind. One of the storks lifts a long black leg and stands on one foot, perhaps out of embarrassment.

Glenda laughs. "Do you even know what vultures look like?" she asks, and Anna says she's never seen one. But Glenda knows this isn't true; turkey vultures fly high over the house all the time. They never alight close up, though, not by swimming pools or on docks. At least, not while Anna's around.

"Well, my love, I'm sorry to say you haven't seen one today. Do you know why?" Glenda's eyes dart from Anna to Val. Neither smiles. "Because those are storks! Wood storks!" She laughs as if she's set the joke up herself. The wonderful thing is that she hasn't. The joke flew in.

"Well, whatever they are, they're hideous," says Val, shaking her head in disgust.

Glenda considers the birds. Indeed, they are not pretty. They have no feathers on their heads and faces, which are cov-ered, instead, with a mottled, reptilian skin. Like the marabou stork that she and Dwight saw on a safari many years ago, when he was posted in Tanzania. The bird was Glenda's favorite sight of the day: five feet tall and hunchbacked, with a face that looked like it was newly, badly burned. It was eating the corpse of a small animal, and its pointed beak and happy bobbing reminded Glenda of those wooden toys that nodded over water glasses—"drinking birds," you called them. Never before had death seemed to her so innocent. The blood on the stork's beak was as red as a candy apple.

"I can see how you mixed them up," Glenda concedes, reaching out to pour Anna a cup of coffee. "They look a little bit like vultures."

Val nods politely, her eyes on the coffee Glenda is pouring. It trickles out of the French press slowly. Anna is resting her cheek in her hand, her plate still covered by her father's newspaper. Glenda sets the coffee before her and folds the newspaper closed. Anna touches neither plate nor cup.

"Do you know," Glenda asks her, "why some birds have bald heads?"

Anna shrugs one shoulder. "Do you mean, storks, like the storks that deliver babies?" she asks, and Glenda doesn't mind that she's ignored her question. She is glad to hear the girl expressing some interest.

"Yes!" Glenda says. "Like those. Except the baby stork is a white stork, and you don't find many of those in Florida. There aren't enough babies." Glenda smiles, but Anna remains expressionless, her face in her hand.

"Where did that stupid idea come from anyway?" she asks no one in particular. "Birds delivering babies." She looks down, as if absentmindedly, and pushes her breakfast plate away.

"Next stop: inpatient," Val says automatically, and Glenda flinches, as if the words are directed at her.

Anna releases a low-pitched whine, but drags the plate back toward herself and begins dispersing the soy sausage with a fork. She's frightened of the idea of the inpatient clinic, but Glenda doesn't think Val should resort to scare tactics. Shouldn't a psychiatrist have some better tricks up her sleeve?

Anna takes after Glenda in being small-boned. Glenda was too narrow-hipped, even, to give birth naturally; Paul was born through a C-section. Glenda resented the scar, which felt like an extra violation, something she had not bargained for. She'd known, of course, that pregnancy would change her body, but she'd believed the changes would be reversible. Dwight loved the scar, though. He kissed it regularly. When Glenda complained about it, he would ask, "What, would you rather have birthing hips?"

Val has birthing hips. At first, Glenda assumed this was why she was fretting herself over Anna's slender frame. Jealousy, Glenda thought, when Val made Anna quit the pool after just a few laps, or when she insisted the girl pour whole milk on her cereal. Glenda made a few jokes about how Val was trying to fatten Anna up, until Val took her aside and explained that this was not a laughing matter. Anna was losing weight, Val insisted, and Val was worried that she might have an eating disorder.

At first, this seemed to Glenda ridiculous, a sign of Val's need to pathologize everything. If Anna had lost a few pounds, surely that could be explained by the fact that she had just moved to a new state, a new climate. But by the time the girl started school in late August, Glenda had to acknowledge that she did not look well. The outlines of her skull are visible, and her shoulder blades jut like wings. Her arms look like something you might see in an infomercial for Third World children, and Glenda never sees her legs anymore, since Anna wears only long pants.

Glenda admits that she doesn't understand it. She doesn't understand why Anna would want to lose weight when she is naturally slender. Val explains the eating disorder as something chemical, an imbalance that needs to be corrected. She has taken the girl to see a host of doctors, who have prescribed a rainbow variety of pills. Anna takes them every morning, sullenly, with a sip of juice. Val insists that these are the correct measures to fix a problem like her daughter's. She is professionally trained to deal with problems like this; she has read the latest studies in the medical journals, which now line the windowsills of Glenda's guest cottage. Glenda, on the other hand, knows nothing. The most she knows about eating disorders is what she's seen on *20/20*.

But Glenda has been watching Anna carefully. She has noticed something in the girl's eyes, which seem to be grasping at something internal, pointed backwards and holding on. Glenda wonders if there may be a way to interrupt this grip in her gaze, to get Anna focused on something outside of herself. To feel the way Glenda did, for instance, watching that marabou stork on safari. Val would probably find the idea ridiculous. "Safaris don't solve chemical imbalances!" she would say. But Glenda can't help wondering. She wants to shatter Anna's focus, drop something before her eyes that forces them to let go.

Anna has broken her soy sausage into crumb-sized bites, which she spears one by one on the prongs of her fork. Then she eats them off individually. "Anna," Val warns. "I'm not kidding."

Glenda wishes Val would be quiet. If they could just stop talking about food for a minute, just stop thinking about food, maybe Anna would forget what she was doing and eat normally. Glenda wonders if she should ask the question again, about why some birds have bald heads. It's a matter of hygiene. Vultures and scavenging storks need to have bald heads so that their feathers don't get clotted with blood. Anna might find that fact interesting.

But before she can speak, Paul emerges from the pool-house, accompanied by the sound, somewhere in the dark behind him, of metal crashing. He is holding a long pole with a net attached to one end. The storks don't wait for him to make a move but take off immediately, swooping down from the roof and out over the pool. Val shrieks. The unfolding of their bodies combined with the thick sound of their wings makes them seem closer than they actually are. Glenda feels as if they're invading the air by her face, like moths suddenly exposed to light.

✿ ✿ ✿

Friday mornings, after breakfast, Glenda walks down to the banyan tree and reads poetry to Dwight. She still calls it reading poetry to Dwight because that was the original idea; after he died, she couldn't tolerate beauty without him. Couldn't see the ripple of sunset expanding from the yolk of sun, couldn't read a line like *a day of dappled sea-borne clouds*, couldn't even listen to Anna's laugh without being wracked with pain. Surely, she thought, there was something else she should be doing? Besides allowing such moments to fill her and fade?

So Friday has become a kind of consolation. Each time she is confronted with something beautiful, she tells herself: Friday, the banyan tree. The banyan tree seemed like the right place because it was where she saw Dwight more awed than she ever had before. It made her laugh. Together, they'd seen many awe-inspiring things—a giant crater, teeming with hippos and gazelle; a palace that appeared to float on a lake; a foggy red-light district where

131

prepubescent girls swayed sedated in windows—and Dwight had moved through them all unfazed. "It's only a job," he liked to say, as he nuzzled her back in their home-scented bed (through eleven countries, their sheets kept the same smell). "I would be just as happy on some farm in Kansas with you."

Florida, it ended up being. Dwight's last post had been the Soviet Union, and after that, they couldn't think of anything better than warmth, color, humidity—a retirement cliché. But Dwight hadn't been lying. He was happy in their little house, never restless like Glenda worried he would be. Which just went to show how well she knew him. This multilingual man who'd dined with kings. Who would've guessed he needed only the radio on the lanai, the tiptoeing of egrets, walks by the bay at sunset? When they found the banyan tree, he slapped his palms against his thighs and let out a hoot. "What in God's name!" They made love in one of the crevices created by the high, gray roots, without lying down, without taking off their clothes. Glenda hadn't realized this was something their bodies could still do.

(Since then, she has learned more about banyans. Not trees, really. Parasites, opportunists, tyrants. She wonders what kind of tree this particular one has strangled. Imagines its shriveled trunk mummified inside the gray drippings.)

Dwight's reaction to the banyan was the kind Glenda would have liked to inspire in him more often. His death did not stop her from trying. The tree became a kind of shrine; each Friday she brought a new gift—a story about Anna, an article, a poem—to send up through the branches on the sound of her voice. But after a few months of this, something unexpected happened. Glenda began to enjoy speaking for the act itself. Her voice sang out between the roots, and she forgot to direct her words at Dwight or anyone. There was less she felt compelled to communicate.

She began bringing books of poetry she doubted Dwight would like, just for the pleasure of hearing herself read them. Dwight had never been much of a fan of poetry to begin with. He knew the ones everyone did, knew enough Shakespeare and Yeats to get around. But Glenda began bringing women poets who'd been angry and died young. She read stanzas that felt like sacrilege, stanzas like *I am too pure for you or anyone./Your body/Hurts me as the world hurts God. I am a lantern*—within the tombs of the banyan tree. Why did it feel so wonderful? Dwight had never hurt her (well, never on purpose, never so much that she'd minded), and she'd never considered herself pure. How Dwight fit into things became such a complicated question that she eventually needed to eliminate, from these readings, any consideration of him. She called it reading poetry to Dwight, but that's not really what it was.

To the banyan today, she's brought Cummings, whom Dwight did, in fact, know some of. The poem ending with *not even the rain has such small hands* he copied into one of her last birthday cards. Because it's true: Glenda has such small hands. She sits in the grass just outside the banyan's shadows and slips off her sandals, wiggling her toes in the spongy grass. The tide is out and a marshy smell wafts off the bay.

Glenda flips the book's soft pages, looking for a poem. It is one that she discovered after Dwight, one that makes her think of life without him. She forgets how it goes, but she will know it when she sees it. Ah, yes! There it is. *"If I have made my lady intricate,"* is how it begins.

She tries the words a few ways. Heavily enunciated, like a Shakespearean actor. Sung to an invented melody. And then shouted, as loud as her worn voice will go:

"Let the world say! His most wise music! Stole nothing! From death!" The words echo under the dome of sky, over flat water, against the walls of the banyan. She pauses, for a moment, in silence, hearing what she has done. And then she laughs, as she does often nowadays.

Dwight could never have been an artist. She knew this when she married him. His practicality, his concreteness were what she loved most about him—the rugged body under the starched fabric of the tuxedo, the rough, boyish face. He made everyone comfortable with his down-home manners, preferred playing the fool to saying something that couldn't be understood by everyone in the room. It was through him she learned that good politicians need not be intelligent, that generosity is what matters. He was the embodiment of a line from Eleanor Roosevelt she learned around that time: "Charm is the ability to forget oneself and become engrossed in other people."

Glenda never forgot herself. Not back then, not when Dwight was working. Which is not to say she wasn't charming; she knew she was, knew how to make it appear like she'd forgotten herself completely, how to hang onto every word of a conversation about rank changes or the economy. But even while she was seemingly engrossed, there was always another part of her, watching herself. She watched herself through other people's eyes, trying different ones on like glasses. But it was Dwight's eyes she came back to more often than not. Through Dwight, she would watch herself laugh, her eyes soften, her charming engrossment in another person. "What a kind, graceful woman," she, as Dwight, would think, and then be filled with happiness.

Sometimes, on those nights, those state dinners, those ambassador balls aglow with yellow light, her beauty felt like a waste. She would feel intoxicated by her effect, her body pushing at the seams of her dress. She'd drink too much, usually, and talk to everyone in the room, although she never, ever, made a scene. By the end of the night, she'd still feel adrift, uncaptured. She never wanted to go home when it was time, and when she finally did, would ask Dwight to make love to her roughly, to hold her arms against the bed. He didn't like doing it this way and it caused fights sometimes between them.

What a lucky woman Eleanor Roosevelt was! For forgetting yourself, Glenda thinks, is not an easy thing. Not once you've had a taste, once you've read one too many romantic sonnets, or seen a film where your quivering lips and watering eyes fill the screen, or fallen in love with a man who watches you walk across a crowded room—after that, it's hard to go back. Hard to go back to being inside yourself, which is too bad, for it's only inside yourself that happiness is possible.

Glenda will tell Anna this, she decides, looking out over the calm bay. She will make sure Anna knows the difference between her eyes and other people's. It seems like such a simple idea, now, when Glenda thinks about it in the bright sunshine, in the warm, sea-scented day. It seems like such a simple idea that Glenda cannot remember, for the life of her, why it took her so many years to learn it.

❈ ❈ ❈

"In Denmark, storks on the roof mean someone in the house is going to die before the end of the year. I read it on Wikipedia."

Anna sits across the kitchen table, behind the "smoothie" Glenda has made her for an after-school snack. Glenda makes the smoothies before Anna gets home, so the girl can't see what goes in them. Blended in this one are two scoops of Häagen Dasz ice cream, a half-cup of whole cream, a heaping handful of raspberries, a heaping handful of chocolate chips, and a banana. Glenda claimed it was mostly fruit.

"You looked up storks on Wikipedia?" Glenda has never seen Wikipedia, but she can infer from the name that it's educational.

"Sure." Anna shrugs. "I look up everything on Wikipedia."

"Really?" Glenda is delighted. "Like what else?"

"Well, I don't remember *now*," Anna says. "You can look up anything on there and find pretty accurate information. Every article gets checked by, like, two hundred people. I don't know why we can't use it for papers. I'd trust an article written by a thousand people more than a book by just one dude." Anna bends her straw up and down with one finger as she speaks. Glenda counts it as a good sign that she's treating the smoothie carelessly. Now, if she'd just be careless enough to drink it.

"Why don't you take a sip?" Glenda asks, nodding toward the glass.

"Why don't *you*?" Anna says, but her voice is soft, and she appears remorseful. Anna doesn't resist Glenda's attempts to feed her in the same way she does her parents'. With her parents, the girl throws borderline tantrums, emptying dishes down the garbage disposal and slamming the door to her room in tears. But with Glenda, she is shyer, more embarrassed.

"That's a good question," says Glenda, who is drinking a cup of tea. She gets up and goes to retrieve a glass. Through the window above the sink, she can see a flight of swallows, swooping in and around the swimming pool.

She sits back down and pours herself a bit of Anna's smoothie. She takes a long sip. The liquid is thick and leaves a cold mustache across her upper lip. She smiles at Anna without making an attempt to wipe it away. They both laugh.

"Now," Glenda says. "Drink and tell me what you learned about storks."

Anna's blue eyes are skeptical. "I'm not so sure what *I* get out of that bargain," she says. "I know *you* want me to drink, and I know *you* want to hear what I learned about storks."

Glenda wants to tell her that it's not a bargain, simply a snack-time conversation. But she doesn't want to seem confrontational. "Well, how's this," she suggests. "For every sip and stork fact, I'll tell you one thing about you I find beautiful." It's a hasty counter-offer; Glenda tells Anna she's beautiful all the time. But to her surprise, the girl accepts, after a moment in which her face darkens defensively. Her expression in that moment seems to Glenda like the kind that might pass over the face of a convict whose crime has been mentioned during a prison visit. But it quickly passes, leaving in its place a sad sort of curiosity.

They begin.

Did Glenda know, Anna asks, that the idea of a baby-carrying stork comes from a myth in which the baby is being not delivered, but stolen? It is the myth of the Pygmy queen, Gerana, who had a body as delicate as a fairy's and a son whom she adored. In her beauty, Gerana was worshipped by the Pygmy people as if she were a goddess, and for this reason, resented real goddesses. She was particularly fond of slandering Artemis, who one day decided to take revenge by turning her into a crane. Devastated at being separated from her son, Gerana swooped down to the land of the Pygmies to scoop up the swaddled infant in her beak. But her husband went at the bird with a stick, forcing her to drop the child. From then on, Gerana hovered always nearby, waiting for another opportunity to steal her child away. She was eventually killed by the Pygmies, which was how Pygmies and cranes became mortal enemies.

"And you know, cranes and storks—birds of a feather." Anna takes a sip of the smoothie and makes an exaggerated gagging sound. "This is *disgusting*."

"Please," Glenda says.

Anna's smile is full and straight and joyful (albeit skeletal now, but Glenda doesn't mention this). Glenda has seen the girl use it to win people over, to make herself an exception. With Paul, especially, who caves to the girl's requests for money and rides without seeming to know what has happened, as if he's been hypnotized.

"You—you have the kind of smile you need to be careful with."

Anna blinks a few times quickly. Takes another sip.

In Egyptian hieroglyphics, the soul was depicted as a human head on a stork's body. The stork travels many miles during the day and returns, always, to the same nest, just like the soul returns to the body after a night of dreams. The Egyptians believed that unborn souls resided in watery places, and that the stork carried these souls to the world of humans, delivering them to their personified forms.

And another sip. Good, then! It's working.

Anna has a smattering of pale freckles across her cheeks and over the bridge of her nose. When she wears a swimsuit, you can see more of these on her shoulders and upper chest. Dwight was marked similarly, with the same translucent, golden skin. Glenda thinks the combination lends Anna a pastoral beauty—the kind that makes you think of sunlight on green hills, of the sound of bells.

Anna's brow is furrowed. She twirls the straw around the inside of the glass.

The Bible lists the stork among the many birds man is not supposed to eat. Included, also, in this list are the eagle, the vulture, the sea gull, the owl, the heron, the bat—

"The bat?"

"I know, not a bird." Anna seems to be getting tired. She takes a short sip. "But those birds were probably forbidden by the Bible because they were dirty. The birds that eat dead stuff and rodents. Which is exactly the reason you wouldn't want to eat a bat." The girl's eyes are wet for some reason, which makes them all the more blue.

"Your eyes," Glenda says. "Oh, Anna, let me tell you about your eyes." Glenda knows how she'll tell it. She wants to describe the hospital room where Anna was born, the curtain between the two beds, the beeping monitors, the doctor's friendly expression over his paper mask. Then the baby's cries, her tight face. To describe how she, Glenda, bent over the bassinet, and how Anna's swollen eyelids opened at that very moment, for the first time.

But Anna is crying. The tears stream suddenly down her cheeks and she makes no effort to wipe them away. "Time-out," she whispers. "I don't want to do this anymore."

Glenda sits still for a moment, her mouth still open. "Oh, Anna," she says again and stretches out her arms. Anna comes around the table and plops herself in Glenda's lap like a little girl. Glenda wraps her arms around her and a few stray tears drop to the sleeve of her sweater.

There is a small bruise on Anna's shoulder, and Glenda, while wondering how it's possible for a person to get a bruise there, kisses it, presses her lips to it hard. "Shhh," she whispers, and Anna's crying grows softer. Glenda remembers, suddenly, something else about storks. The raspberry veins, found in a newborn's eyelids—or sometimes on the bridge of the nose—called "stork bites."

Glenda catches one of Anna's hands in her own. "Your fingers are so long and slender," she sighs, running her own hand over them. "How I always wished mine could be."

❊ ❊ ❊

The sunset that night is a deep crimson, inflaming the shallows of the bay. In the red water stand the silhouettes of egrets. They're stalking the schools of fish that run so thick this time of year you can't watch the water for more than a minute without seeing one leap helplessly against the sky.

Val has prepared a dinner of couscous and raisins, which the family eats on the lanai. Glenda drinks white wine to soothe her muscles, which ache on the days when she walks to the banyan and back. Anna is quietly using her fork to mash her food. After their conversation that afternoon, the girl disappeared into her room for hours. Now, she seems clammy and not quite awake. The hot-looking sky produces a chill in Glenda's aching muscle—it's the left leg that's bothering her lately, a pain that starts in the calf and runs up the thigh.

"T-G-I-F," announces Paul, finishing off his wine. He is barely touching the couscous, and Glenda knows this is because he does not like it. A life spent abroad has instilled Paul with very American tastes. He prefers meat and potatoes, but rarely gets them because Val cooks vegetarian for Anna. When Glenda does the cooking, she makes Paul a separate dinner, a steak or pork chop along with whatever she's preparing for the rest of them. It isn't really any extra trouble. A few minutes, at the most.

"Was it a busy week?" Glenda asks to fill the silence following Paul's remark. He and Val say so little to each other at the dinner table that Glenda sometimes wonders whether they would eat dinner together at all were they not living in her house.

"It was a madhouse," says Paul, reaching for the wine bottle. "An absolute madhouse."

"That must be nice," Val says.

Paul looks like he is about to respond but ends up (wisely, Glenda thinks) ignoring the comment. Paul is a dermatologist, which means he's had no trouble finding work in Sarasota. Retired people need dermatologists more than they need psychiatrists.

"Anyone else need more wine?" Paul asks, refilling his glass.

"Yes, please," Anna says.

He laughs. "You can't have more wine if you haven't had any to start with."

"You can't have more anything if you haven't had any to start with," says Val, frowning at her daughter's plate.

Glenda finishes off the last drops in her glass and hands it over to Paul. "Who was your most exciting patient?" she asks him.

Val snorts, and they all look at her. "I'm sorry," she says sincerely. "I'm just really interested to hear what you'll say. Was it the Botox for Mrs. Smith? The basal cell on Mr. X?"

Paul just smiles sadly. "I'd actually rather not talk about work, Mom," he says, handing Glenda back a full glass. "If that's okay."

"Of course it's okay!" Glenda takes a sip of wine. "Well, then, what should we talk about?"

No one answers. Anna takes a bite of couscous, and they all watch her chew it with the same surprised expression.

"Ew," she says.

Glenda interjects before Val can ruin the moment. "Anna found out some interesting facts about storks, today," she says. Val and Paul continue looking at their daughter, surprised.

"Storks?" Paul asks.

"Yeah," Anna says. "Like the ones you chased off the roof."

"Oh." Paul looks confused. "I thought they were vultures."

"No, they were wood storks," Anna says. "But there's a reason you got them mixed up. They both eat corpses. That's why they have bald heads."

Val makes a face but continues listening. "I'm sorry," Paul says. "*Why* is that why they have bald heads?"

Anna becomes animated as she explains, still holding her fork in one hand. The sun sinks into the water, casting the lanai in a dark, rosy glow. Anna, Glenda thinks, is better than her parents. She is more talkative and social than Paul, more relaxed and attractive than Val. Glenda sometimes looks at the girl in amazement, wondering where she came from. Lately, she has even started to wonder whether her life has not been a long rehearsal—a rehearsal for loving Anna. This girl from whom she neither expects nor wants anything, except that she should continue to exist. It makes sense that such a pure, uncomplicated love should only come now, at the end of things.

Glenda's heart begins to pound as Anna talks about storks and corpses and mythology. She tries to latch onto what the girl is saying, but her words swirl together against the fading light, the new, plum sky. It is the wine; sometimes it has this effect. All Glenda can focus on is Anna's face, her bright eyes and golden cheeks, the way she waves her fork beside her like a wand. Glenda's heart keeps pounding—too fast; her hand trembles as she sets her glass down.

"I—," she begins, and realizes, too late, that she has interrupted. She has interrupted her granddaughter, talking passionately! Anna pauses, waiting to hear what Glenda will say. Paul and Val are looking at her, too.

What? What is it? Her mouth hangs open like an idiot's.

"I love you!" The words burst forth from her chest and her heart is calm again. She thinks she sees Anna roll her eyes, and wants to laugh. "All of you," she says, using her hand to indicate the whole table. "I love all of you."

Paul reaches his hand out over the table but not far enough to reach hers. "We love you, too, Mom." His voice is soft, with worry or surprise. Val is looking at her as if she might be a new psychiatric patient.

"I'm sorry, Anna," Glenda apologizes, looking back at her granddaughter. "Please—please go on." And the girl picks up where she left off, while the adults watch and listen.

✻ ✻ ✻

After putting on her nightgown and her night cream, Glenda goes barefoot down the hall to Anna's room. A yellow light glows in the crack between the frame and the door, casting a pale strip across the carpet. Glenda says Anna's name softly. There is silence.

Glenda nudges open the door. Anna—still dressed in her unnecessary layers of clothing: sweatshirt and leggings and legwarmers—is sprawled out over the covers, taking up far more space than she does in waking life. Spiraling airily from the ceiling are the garlands she makes from paper flowers, ribbons, beads. Her walls are mostly bare; Anna is quite fastidious about what she puts on them. Hanging now are only a full-length mirror and two pictures—one, a magazine cutout of a man Glenda doesn't recognize but who she thinks might be on drugs; the other, a Hopper print of a woman sitting on a bed bright with sunlight. Glenda thinks the bed might be in a hotel room, though she thinks this about most of Hopper's indoor paintings. The scenes all seem so empty, transient. A little like Anna's room, were it not for the cluttered streams of color dangling from the ceiling, in such plentitude that it has occurred to Glenda that the mobiles might be something of an obsession.

She sits down on the narrow strip of bed not occupied by Anna's tangled limbs. The girl is dreaming—her eyelids flutter and her mouth twitches at one corner. Glenda curls herself up on the narrow strip of bed, makes herself small beside Anna's unconscious expansion.

This is the opposite of how she felt with Dwight, Glenda thinks, as she keeps her body small and frozen beside her granddaughter, despite the discomfort in her muscles. When Dwight slept, Glenda felt abandoned, betrayed somehow. She envied the peace of his unconscious face, and sometimes "accidentally" woke him, or went to great lengths to keep him awake. It seemed unfair to her that he should get this, too, this easy sleep on top of his easy consciousness throughout the day. Now, there's nothing she wants more than for Anna to continue sleeping, to watch the peaceful expression on her sweet face.

Of course, Glenda wanted to keep Paul asleep when he was an infant, too, but that was also different from how she feels with Anna. That was sheer exhaustion, a desperation for silence, for herself. Glenda wouldn't have minded, though, if Anna were awake when she came into her room. That was, after all, her purpose in coming: to tell the girl something before she went to bed.

What does she want to tell her? It seems everything and nothing all at once. She wants to tell her about the safari in Tanzania, the hippos and the gazelle. She wants to tell her about Dwight, his career and their travels, his surprise at the banyan tree. Anna didn't get to know Dwight very well. Not as well as she is getting to know Glenda.

But most of all, Glenda wants to tell Anna about Anna, herself. She knows the way the girl sees herself is wrong. But Glenda hasn't done a good job, so far, in correcting her. Why did she do that, earlier that day; why did she enumerate the ways in which Anna is beautiful? Those aren't the kinds of things the girl needs to hear. Surely, Anna's just as aware of her beauty as she's aware of the part of herself—still deep inside but hungry and invincible and there—that will eventually destroy that beauty, that will make her old. This, after all, is the only thing to fear.

And once you no longer feared it? Glenda wants to tell Anna what happens then, but she doesn't want to wake her. And so she lies silently beside her and tells the story, from the beginning, in her mind. She and Dwight were in town for Anna's birth, for the whole last month of Val's pregnancy. Glenda remembers the sleek sterility of the hospital, the doctor's apt hands. And then: something glowing, passed to a bassinet in a corner of the room, where it radiates light and heat. Something warm and red, which Glenda can't see, yet, but toward which she is moving . . .

In the dream Anna is dreaming, she's wrapped in a sling that swings from the beak of a giant stork, soaring far above the earth. She can feel the bird's breath on her face, hot and fishy. The sky is black and starless, and when she looks down, she sees that land has disappeared. Earth is a liquid ball, glowing blue, spinning through space, as in the beginning of time.

The History of Ecstasy

—*"The Ecstasy of St. Francis," Caravaggio*

Everything in freefall through the trees,
Blue-phloxed & dahliaed as they land,
the flowers we see like sunspots after we close
our eyes. The heart of the wren has an oculus
that lets in only rain, or so its song tells us,
& you've meditated on it so long, the acetylene
milk-starred wren's heart, nine-sided & sailed,
you hear the rustling of its wings each time the drops
begin to fall. In the dark each night the carillonneur
of starlight begins to play, the same two tones
pulsing endlessly, the song of the burning shirt,
the dark buttonhole the nipple slips through.
Where in the tendons & slender muscles
is that memory stored, that has her hands
on that first chord without noticing when she
sits before the keys? Like a dowser staring
at Sahara sand, hands trembling. It's a love
passed down in the bones that has people,
even under gunfire, taking the time to bury
their saints' relics beneath the second willow
at the river's edge. It's something passed
from her mother that has my mother awake
most of the night, trying a last glass of port,
Tylenol 3, chamomile, tryptophan, & finally
Ambien, a bell-sound always between her & sleep.
And so the Italians discover Caravaggio
in their blood, that heart so full of terrible echoes,
the history of the ecstasy of St. Francis
in their palm prints. Though paradise might mean
unbridled joy, who can say if we'd know it when

we found it, or if we'd find our way back again—
the same ecstasy might be somewhere in our own,
if we're willing to bear the wounds. I know by the ache
that water is rising from the soil,
that storms will soon race over the ridgeline
into the valley, each about the size of the town
I grew up in, each with a day's worth of water if it fell
only into each of our palms, spilling into each corner
of our lives. Listen: the sound of wings, the peace that sleep
follows, small mercies, the first drops beginning to fall.

Anne Thompson, photograph

Mothman's Guide to the Here & Hereafter

The history of flight began with hollow bones
& starlight, & before that? Membranes of hammered dust
& dew, landing spots on clover, on the white ziggurats
of Queen Anne's Lace. The slaves that built the temples
& railroads buried their dead beneath the stones & rails—
beneath the ties that bled tar in the sun, dirt & traces
of nitroglycerin atop them, stamped flat by bare feet—
so they became monuments to the dead of the captives.
All language is survival, from hieroglyphs to the green neon
on a highway overpass, the tag of someone who's watched
the city for a long time from a fire escape. Once it was leeches
& maggots for your wounds. Now it's iodine to help with
the radioactivity, saltwater mixed with boron to cool
the reactor. All language is the revelation of our essence
& where it fails, one finds human chains: hand to foot repeated
a thousand times, draped across the graffiti & concrete of Dresden
to commemorate the firebombing. When the daughters
of the Argentinian exiles draw people climbing into helicopters,
they draw them with wings, because they remember the whispered
stories about the disappeared, who were thrown out in chains
over rivers. *Desaparecidos.* Early radar operators couldn't explain
the "ghost chatter" on their green screens, migrating geese
or cloud cover or moondogs, here then gone, maybe echoes,
wakes they might have tracked to the kingdom of the dead.
Even now amateurs in uncounted countries are following
military aircraft as best they can, using tail numbers & call signs,
listening over unencrypted UHF & VHF radio, & plotting
the flights on a map, each landing spot one possible
vanishing point of the rendered. Prayer is the essence
of language, the revelation of our need. That's why it's possible
to hear the sighed anaphoras in lovemaking as a kind of rosary—
a sweep of neck, the unnamed hollows, a ribcage like a pagoda
of pear blossoms. Once it was laurel for your youth,
your hand smoothing the spots & scars on another's back:
the same wakes followed more closely. I wish I could
promise that you'll take that image with you when
you go. Look closer: trace a constellation

of small parachutes drifting above the Helmand River
& across the poppy fields in bloom beside it—
a constellation traced by the farmer looking up
at them—parachutes slowing the descent of metal
canisters, each with a star packed inside. Like the poppies.
Like each wound, each body. When you see the burnlines
of firepits in a new henge found in a farmer's field,
think of your need, think of the eyespots on the smallest wings.

From the collection of the Managing Editor, photograph

Another Dinner Party

Have one samosa, one at least," said Lalitha Arora, holding out the plate as she tipped her body in a cartoonish bow.

"One samosa, I could eat ten samosas!" said Baskar, the man lounging next to Shilpa on the couch, but he took only one.

Shilpa didn't think anybody could eat ten samosas, especially not these made by Lalitha Arora, or Lala, as she insisted everybody call her. But that was a harsh thought, so she took it back and took a samosa, too, just to see Lala's face lighting up at the lighter plate.

Unlike most aunties, Lala couldn't cook at all. She thought she could, and it would have made more sense if she could have, since she hosted an Indian healthy cooking radio show called "Eating with Aunty." The problem was that she liked to improvise. When Shilpa had first arrived at Lala's house, the aunty had sat her down in the living room next to Baskar and described the recipe to them both in great detail. This time, she had baked the samosas rather than frying them and she'd replaced the usual potato filling with a puree of vegetables she declared more nutritional, such as swiss chard and broccoli, which, after being swirled in the blender, had become really too watery to hold up the samosa's triangular shape.

Shilpa heard Baskar's teeth crunch over something as he chewed and she hoped it was cumin. The two of them and Shilpa's children were the only guests so far, although the party had technically started an hour earlier. Lala's husband hovered roundly in the background rooms, waiting for a good time to introduce himself, even though any time would have been fine. He peered out at them and smiled from various doorways, and eventually came out and said hello.

"Hello!" he said, "I am Lala's husband!"

Nobody thought to ask for his name. He beamed at Baskar. He bowed exactly as his wife had and took Shilpa's hand, kissing it lightly and off-center, then darted away like a woodland creature.

❊ ❊ ❊

Shilpa had met the older woman three months earlier, at Ashwin's funeral. Lala's party was the first social gathering Shilpa had attended since then. Perhaps, she thought, I should have waited longer.

Partly she'd come because Lala had cajoled her, but mostly she'd just become sick of her house, now full of all her packed-up belongings. She and the kids were moving houses to save money; in a week they'd unpack again in a shrunken space. The part she dreaded was deciding what to toss. For now, she skipped those decisions, wrapping even the useless items — a hazardously broken toaster oven, sunglasses she didn't wear — in sheets from *The Toronto Star*.

Hindu custom said to avoid celebrations for a year after the death of a spouse; it was believed to take one year for the soul to reach God. And maybe she should have respected that, but that morning she'd woken up on her queen-sized mattress, having placed it on the floor after dismantling the bed frame, and looked up to towers of boxes on each side of her, and thought for an alarming second that she saw them shift. They were all different sizes (picked up free from an appliance store), and she hadn't been careful about placement. It was possible, perhaps, that a settling object could unsettle the balance enough for a series of boxes to fall and crush her in her sleep. Ravi would find her in the morning and scream, waking up baby Mira, who would roll around, full of anguish, in her crib.

So she'd come to the party for a break from boxes and bare walls, and to please Lala, who had known Ashwin for several years. He had been a chemical engineer, and she had interviewed him once on her show. Lala never lost contact with a single person she had a conversation with. She invited bank tellers out to lunch with her and, after meeting the Canadian Prime Minister's wife once at a cultural conference, had obtained her home phone number.

Shilpa had never been to her house before; they'd mostly just gone on cheap lunch outings to Udupi Palace, Lala's favorite South Indian restaurant, which served the exact same dishes Shilpa made at home every day. Lala's home décor seemed to mimic the restaurant's. On the wall she'd placed ornate plaster carvings that looked much heavier than they were, portraying Indian dancers with imprecise faces, noses placed too high and mouths that smirked too readily. Stainless steel dishware crowded onto glass shelves around the room, underlit with neon pink light. A pewter salt-and-pepper set in the corner nearest to Shilpa identically matched the shakers at Udupi Palace. There was also an oil painting of a wobbly-looking bowl of fruit, which Lala told them she had done herself. It was so tall and so wide that, rather than hanging it, Lala had stood the painting on the floor, after pushing aside the red IKEA furniture to make room.

Gradually, more guests started to arrive. Lala offered to take their coats even though it was summer and nobody had any coats. "May I take your jacket?" she asked one woman in a fitted sleeveless selwar kameez.

"Ohhh, Lala, you and your jokes!" the woman said.

A few of the guests were radio folk and some were neighbors, others colleagues of Lala's husband, who taught Hindi classes at the university. Some guests seemed entirely arbitrary, like Baskar, who turned out to be a manager at a factory that made computer ink, and couldn't remember how he had met the Lalas at all. "Here or there," he said to Shilpa when she asked. Baskar balanced his quarter-eaten samosa on his napkin, almost dropping it when Shilpa explained that she'd met Lala at her husband's funeral. "Oh, I'm very sorry," said Baskar, and moved exactly one centimeter away from her on the sofa, so their legs no longer touched. Shilpa felt infinite relief, because Baskar wore appalling, frayed, bulky jeans—to a dinner party!—and she remembered Ashwin's perfectly ironed pants and how she'd once caught him doing a sitting-down test to make sure his stomach didn't bulge in them and that the hems didn't rise and reveal too much of his socks.

Maybe twenty people had arrived, and more kept coming.

"It has been a thousand-million years since we have seen one another!" exclaimed Lala to one extremely thin woman. Lala had a habit of hyperbolizing time, of exaggerating a few days into millions of years, and this habit gave such greetings and many of her anecdotes a fairy-tale beauty. Lala embraced the woman, whose elbows pointed out like warped branches.

Shoes piled up near the entrance and a few diligent youngsters began moving the surplus to the laundry room.

"Not mine!" said one old man, shaking his head amiably at a girl who tried to nab his loafers before he'd even removed them. "I need the support of my orthotics." The girl moved on to the next pair and the man wore his shoes for the rest of the evening, happily trampling many other people's feet, socked and bare.

"Sit down, sit down," said Lala, guiding the ladies and men into the living room. Two more people crammed on to the sofa with Shilpa and Baskar—suddenly their legs were touching again—and four more pulled chairs from the dining room and arranged them nearby. Lala had scattered an assortment of candy-colored cushions around the floor as extra seating. The guests crossed their legs or pulled their knees to their chests or searched the other rooms for chairs (depending on whether they'd worn skirts or pants or Indian clothes), and some stood seatlessly in between, so there were four levels of heads—floor sitters, sofa sitters, chair sitters, and standers—like the distinct layers of trees in a rainforest. Some children, including Ravi, bounced around like frogs. Shilpa had left little Mira sleeping in the guest room.

Lala moved through the guests offering her plates of samosas and crackers and a lumpy pumpkin paté. She brought out sparkling bottles of pomegranate and mango juice and poured them scarlet and yellow into glasses of various odd heights. "We have wine, too!" she exclaimed, and everybody looked around excitedly because none of them ever drank wine.

Lala's husband handed out napkins at his wife's request. When he'd finished, he went nimbly from one end of the room to the other and then to the adjacent rooms, turning lamps and light switches on and off. After each switch, he stopped and looked at Lala, as though considering which tones of light made her look best.

The thin elbowy woman began a conversation with Shilpa.

"Do you listen to Lala's show?" the woman asked.

"Every Sunday morning," Shilpa said, thinking of the many Sunday mornings, not many, but fourteen, exactly, when Mira had sucked at her bottle and looked sleepily at Shilpa from her high chair, when Ravi had lain on his stomach in the hallway, silently drawing pictures, the crayon patterns taking up the grain of the wood floor, and Shilpa had turned the volume way up so Lala's voice would fill the house and make it feel less empty.

"You know, her recipes turn out pretty well when you make them yourself," said the woman.

"Have you tried the samosas?" asked Shilpa.

"Oh yes, they are awful, aren't they? One time," she confided, "Lala made some kind of sweet. We couldn't tell what sweet it was supposed to be, and I think she'd used Splenda, but you know you can't use anything but sugar with Indian sweets, and anyway they were so hard we couldn't bite them, and you know what my son told me he did? He said he just tossed it up in the air—in the air!—and didn't even check to see where it landed. Somewhere in this house, there is an unidentifiable sweet, rotting under a table or inside a plant." They both giggled and then the woman fell awkwardly silent. They took large bites of their samosas when Lala came around.

"Stop eating those samosas," said Lala. "It's dinner time!"

Everybody who had been there before cringed. A line formed at the food table. Shilpa checked on Mira (half-asleep, not hungry), then collected Ravi and went to the very back of the line. Somebody handed them plates. The table was set with a teal tablecloth and dotted with candles that kept being nearly knocked over. The foods didn't seem to be Indian, but rather sort of fusion concoctions in swampy shades of brown and green.

"Is this a lasagna?" asked a short man with a booming voice that Shilpa recognized from the Hindi music radio program.

"Ahh, not quite," said Lala, serving him a gigantic amount. "It's more of a savory pie."

"Yum, I love banana bread," said a woman with a blue hat, as Lala placed a piece on her plate.

"That's actually a lentil loaf," said Lala.

The doorbell rang then, but nobody answered it. The door opened and a woman stood there in a full silk saree, seeming unsure of whether to enter. Lala dropped the serving spoon she was holding and hurried to the door.

"Come in, my dear," she said, "You've been a hundred hours standing on this porch." In three seconds, she had taken the woman's imaginary coat and ushered her to the front of the food line. She loaded the woman's plate without speaking.

Shilpa helped Ravi get his food, arranging items pleasingly around his plate, which might help ensure he ate them. He went to sit in another room, one that had a television, with several other children. While Shilpa helped Ravi, Lala packed Shilpa's plate with far more food than she would have taken herself.

"Don't be shy, come have more!" said Lala.

"I will, it all looks so good," said Shilpa.

She balanced the plate in one hand and picked up a glass of water from the clear row of glasses at the end of the table. Turning around to go back to the sofa, she was careful not to tilt her plate and drop food on the heads of people who sat around her legs. But after she turned, she saw that the late-arriving woman had usurped her seat on the sofa. The chairs and floor cushions were all taken. People shared cushions, their backs meeting. Some squashed together on armchairs, and others suspended themselves, feet waving, on the soft red arms of the sofa. She didn't know anybody well enough to share seating, and nobody sat on the bare carpet, and Shilpa didn't think she should, because she knew Lala would make a cute worried fuss about there not being enough places, which would draw attention to her, and she didn't want that.

So Shilpa would have to stand. But how would she eat? Both of her hands were full, making the maneuvering impossible unless she put something down. The only possible table on which to leave her water was the coffee table near the sofa, inconveniently low, and she couldn't stand there because there wasn't any room in between the mismatched wood dining set chairs and the metal folding chairs and she would have to make awkward conversation with the sitting people. They'd look up at her and ask her to repeat herself. If somebody told a joke, Shilpa's laughter would float over their heads.

She couldn't keep her water on the floor next to her, due to the carpet, and even without carpeting, it was likely the glass would be knocked over by an errant child. Even if she could find a place to keep her water, she wasn't sure she could hold the plate in one hand the whole time while eating—Lala had run out of the Corelle and broken out the china, which was too heavy to hold for long—and she had a fork and a spoon balanced on the plate along with a napkin tucked uncomfortably in her palm. Lala had given her so much food that it threatened to topple, plus, because the food was so unappetizing, she didn't know how she would subtly hide what she wasn't eating and so she would be forced to eat it all.

What were other people doing? Shilpa looked at the standers. They formed a tight corner circle. How would she talk to them? She hadn't met a single one of them before. To join the group, she would need to tap somebody on the shoulder, or stand sideways until somebody noticed her, and there wasn't even room there to stand. Even to get over there she would have to walk around several cushion-seated people, and would probably crush somebody's child under her feet.

If Ashwin were here, such a dilemma would not have existed, because, first of all, he would have saved her a seat or she would have saved him a seat, or he would have told her to leave her selwar shawl where they were sitting, or to keep her purse on the chair.

Or they might have stood and shared plate and glass, minimizing the amount of food they would have to eat and coordinating into a lovely and precise symbiosis. She remembered a time when they had done this before. Ashwin held the plate in two hands while Shilpa clutched the glass in one hand and used her other hand to eat.

"Don't touch the mysore pak, that's my favorite," he said, and she didn't know if he was joking or not.

"Crumbs, I will leave you crumbs," she responded, holding the sweet up to her mouth and threatening to eat it whole. Then she took a tiny corner bite, barely touching it with her teeth. She saved it for him on the very edge of the dish, where it wouldn't be tainted with the residue of other foods.

"Oh, I was joking, you can eat it," he said, and then she didn't know if he was just being generous. She picked it up again but before she could repeat her silly pantomime, he suddenly dipped his head forward, nearly dropping the plate, and bit the piece of mysore pak out of her hand, as though it were an offered grape.

They often compared foods to other foods. "This is the biggest chappati I've ever seen!" Shilpa had heard Ashwin say, and she'd also heard him exclaim, "This chappati is impossibly soft!" and, "This chappati is even more delicious than my mother's!" (he was overwhelmingly positive in his opinions, at least while expressing them at dinner parties, to aunties who simpered under his handsomeness). They attended a dinner party every weekend, sometimes twice a weekend. They had an incredibly large social circle. Sometimes they went to lunch parties as well. On the drive home, husband and wife always critiqued the meal together: "Did that one curry taste exactly like that other curry?" Ashwin asked.

"All curries taste the same," said Shilpa.

"It's the MTR powder, probably."

Then they both gazed out the dark front windshield on to the highway that led them home from Mississauga to Richmond Hill. When they passed the Vishnu temple near their exit, they both touched the dashboard in prayer.

One of them would bring up the time they had eaten at MTR—the Mavalli Tiffin Room—in Bangalore, only a few days after they had first met. They'd gone to Lal Bagh Road and stepped into the crowded restaurant, where patrons tucked into meals brimming out of stainless steel sectioned plates. The place wasn't beautiful, but it was the most famous restaurant in India.

"Once, the Chief Minister of Karnataka himself stood in line here to have a masala dosa," Ashwin told her outside the restaurant.

"I know that, everybody in the whole state of Karnataka knows that," she said.

"You are charming," he said, very seriously, and she laughed aloud because she had only ever heard the word "charming" in the novels of Jane Austen.

They ordered crisp paper dosas, which came to them folded into half-moons, stuffed with cumin-scented yellow potatoes cooked until they'd lost their shape. The surface of the dosa glistened with oil that highlighted the crepe's gradual gradient from white to brown, darker where it had touched the center of the pan. Shilpa raised her eyebrows at him, at his boyish, asymmetrical face, throwing her eyes over the dosas and the steel plates and their messy, potato-covered hands. The faux-marble tabletop seemed like real marble. She said his name in the middle of some forgettable sentence, and thought the name Ashwin sounded like a combination of a sneeze and a sigh.

On the way out of MTR, Ashwin had put his hand for one second on the small of her back and Shilpa had tensed. Ashwin had thought he was being too forward, and apologized. They grinned about that moment later, after they'd crossed the Atlantic. In their suburban Canadian house, they watched television in their bedroom, stayed up late as though they needed to feel guilty about it (Ashwin's head on Shilpa's stomach, folded over each other in their bed like resting cows), watching the Fox Network as though it had been banned.

❊ ❊ ❊

They would fall asleep with the television still on, and it flashed over their sleeping bodies until morning. Ashwin would wake up and stretch and say, "Strrrrrretch!" his mouth open and his eyes closed and his arms reaching up and over Shilpa, purposely waking her so he could cuddle her with more results. She would blink into his cheek and ask, "Why can't you stretch without saying the word 'stretch'?"

He would eventually get up to shower, turning the TV off as he passed it, and after ten minutes, Shilpa would listen to hear him get out of the shower and say aloud to himself, "Cleaaann as a whistle!" She would smother her laughing reaction with the Ashwin-flattened pillow, after rolling to his side of the bed, where the sheets were warm as a fresh roti; she would wait there in the space he had left.

❊ ❊ ❊

Here she was now, back in the cycle of more dinner parties, unsure of how to eat, still in the limbo of holding her plate and glass. She had never had neurotic problems like these before. Ashwin had always had a plan for such situations. They had glided through without Shilpa ever needing to worry about where to sit, where to set down her glass, where to find parking, where to find a reliable moving company, where to mail the completed tax forms, where to enroll Ravi in daycare, where to hold a funeral, where to keep her dead husband's Great Dad mug, in the cupboard, and let the kids drink from it, or in some kind of Ashwin shrine, or should she keep it in a storage container in their new basement for ten years before letting Mira and Ravi open it like a gift—here, here is your father in this box.

❊ ❊ ❊

Shilpa retreated to the kitchen. The water in her glass rippled as she set it down on the countertop. Lala was in there, washing silverware.

"You still haven't eaten, what is this?" Lala asked, pointing at Shilpa's plate with a handful of forks.

Shilpa, still thinking of Ashwin's face over the MTR table, couldn't quite answer.

"Shilpa, what is wrong?"

"Missing Ashwin," she said, two words being the most words possible.

She remembered how Ashwin had added yogurt to everything he ate.

Lala put her forks down and touched Shilpa's back with her palm. "Don't worry, *beta*," she said, her North Indianness emerging through the endearment. Shilpa began crying, and the aunty held her whole body tightly in the bend of her elbow.

Shilpa saw Lala's husband enter the kitchen. His white hair frizzed from the humidity of the cooking and all the bodies. She saw him pause, look to the wall at his left, and quietly turn off the first switch in the row of three kitchen lights.

❊ ❊ ❊

"Who is that?" Shilpa asked Lala about the woman in her sofa seat, after they had dried the silverware.

"Who, Baskar? Didn't I introduce you?"

"No, that lady there," she pointed quickly with her chin, through the kitchen entrance.

"Oh, she's a neighbor," said Lala vaguely.

The woman seemed unconcerned with the social situation going on around her—she ate silently, listening only superficially to Baskar rattle on, probably about manufacturing toner—but rather seemed focused on the task of balancing her plate on her lap, making sure the liquids on the plate didn't drip off the side. She was about ten years older than Shilpa, very carefully put together; her saree kept immaculate pleats, fanned outward at the bottom over painted toenails and three silver toe rings. Her face had a definite oval shape, emphasized by her middle-parted hair, and her eyebrows were almost too dark, except in comparison with her eyes. She was beautiful, but seemed persistently very near to tears.

"And what's her story?"

"Her story—," Lala started, stopped, started again. "Her husband died last week."

"Last week?"

"She was all alone at home, so I invited her. I didn't really think she would come. He was ill for such a long time," Lala said, and told her the details of his suffering.

Now, in Lala's living room, the woman was eating rice, soaked in the leakings of pie. Shilpa had temporarily stopped eating rice at home—a remarkable feat for her—because it always made her recall the last time she had fed rice to Ashwin, at his funeral. The Hindu priest had given her a dish of uncooked, translucent grains, and she had taken a few and placed them into Ashwin's parted, dead mouth.

"Food for the journey," the priest had whispered to her. Then he had given her a silver dropper of water, scented with holy tulsi leaves, and she had carefully let three drops fall over his lips. "To ensure the soul goes straight to God," the priest said, before closing the coffin lid, before men carried the coffin away to the ovens.

"She had him buried; I'm not sure why," said Lala. "It was my first time at such an outdoor-type funeral."

The reason Hindus weren't buried was that they believed cremation destroyed the material link of the body to the soul.

The woman took a bite of wheat noodles, her wrist giving a double-jointed bend. She bit into a piece of the heavy, dry cake of lentils, and pieces crumbled down the sides of her face.

At a wedding, the priest wouldn't say anything about death parting a pair—not in the strings of monotonous Sanskrit prayer—but in the *Lagna Vivah* ceremony, he would join their souls. Sometimes it all sounded like such crap to Shilpa now. But her own wedding program sheets, which she and Ashwin had hand-folded and placed parallel on a hundred white and gold chairs, had explained the steps of the ceremony in neat serif type. The notes said the bride's forehead would be marked with the red circular sign of luck, a sign that her husband would always be with her, only instead of the word "husband," they had typed the word "soul," italicized, one letter leaning into the next like a shoulder to a shoulder.

"Baskar is recently divorced, and is living out of a suitcase at the Days Inn," said Lala. "The man wearing the blazer just moved here but his wife was refused a visa and is stuck in India." She went down the guest list like a roll call. "That woman's son went missing two years ago," said Lala, gesturing at the thin elbowy woman Shilpa had spoken to earlier. "He was abducted at the Square One Mall."

Shilpa wondered whom Lala had lost, and how she had become the nucleus to this strange group of fractured families, and why Lala was pointing out these people to her. Perhaps she intended to diminish Shilpa's pain, and she had diminished its importance, in a too truthful, everybody-has-their-problems way, but Shilpa did not want her grief divided and shared. All she craved then was to be pitied as though hers were the only suffering in the room. She imagined the room crowded with the souls of everyone's missing family members. They paused next to loved ones, held invisible conversations, ate the inedible chutney, and wandered, taking up the few remaining spots of empty carpet space.

Ravi came up to Shilpa, held his still-filled plate right up to her knees. She took the plate from him. Ravi went and sat on a cushion in Shilpa's sight, wiped his hands on the carpet. Maybe, she thought, it is possible to be reincarnated as something inanimate, and after disappearing in the silt of cremation, I will come back renewed, as a coat rack or a napkin, a pair of shoes, a grain of rice.

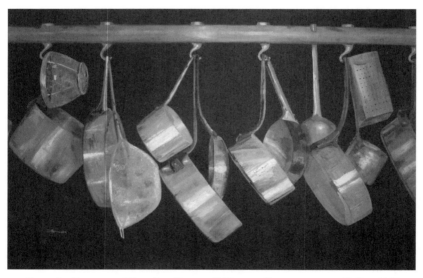

Connie Bryson, *Hanging Pots and Pans*, oil on canvas, 24" x 36"

Inside the Blue Mosque, Istanbul

Say the word aloud, say *blue*,
and the mind teems with guests:
Renoir, Vermeer, Gainsborough's *Blue Boy*,
Picasso's Blue Period, the lines
from a Mark Doty crab poem:
a shocking Giotto blue.

Say *blue*, and a marlin taildances on the water,
a slide guitar spells heartache in plural.
Woke up this mornin', I believe I'll dust my broom.
Frida lives on in *la Casa Azul*.
And the beggar trapped in a hash dream
haze hails bands of blue men from the Sahara.

Say *blue*, and doors swing wide open.
To speak it here adds yet another
tile to the thousands already present.
Did Gershwin divine such a rhapsody?
Such a dazzling faïence mosaic?
Or is blue encoded in our cells,

a script for the primal color of being?
Look around. When you left your shoes
at the door, didn't you slough off
your skin so blue could breathe,
could curl phantom-like among the pillars,

a counterpoint
to the slow, steady rhythm
of a cobbler tapping out his blood
beat in the bazaar, circa 1650?
Blue. It haunts the back alleys,

a companion for the road, for the long haul,
for daughter and courtesan a final recumbent address.
First water, last silence, the country in between.
Blue Danube. Blue bayou. *Cordon bleu*.
The heron and the kingfisher. Blue.

Girlfriend

Miss Claude's own house has gone way downhill. It needs everything from a new roof to new glass and bars on the upstairs windows, now the neighborhood's got so bad. Rain and squirrels get in up there, but I guess it's her house. She has lived a pretty long time.

Miss Claude herself always talks like she's about to bite it. She wants me to feel sorry for her. Not that she's the least bit sorry for me. But there's no one else to listen, take her for a walk, go to the corner store, and not forget about her, which I wouldn't. She'll hold her side and drop a remark about how I must take this or that because she won't last much longer. The Civil War sword over the mantel, or a wooden radio with tubes, like that. But I'm responsible on my own without anyone twisting my arm. (Joke.) I always do my two days a week after school. She perks up when I come in, the rest of the stuff just washes over the top of my head.

Someone comes in, mornings, but no one ever answers the door when I get there after school. I let myself in. That particular day I found her with the covers pulled up to her chin, her face as white as a sheet of paper. Like some old love letter, balled into a million creases.

She was pretending to be asleep. "Oh, napping," I whispered, loud enough for her to hear. I started to back out.

The eyes opened in a nanosecond, "Not so fast. Bring me a glass of water, Young Allen. It's this infernal backache, probably a kidney. I haven't taken a morsel today."

Miss Claude always calls me Young Allen, even though I'm sixteen years old. That's to distinguish me from my grandfather, old Allen, who she knew. They were neighbors in the old days when everyone around here went to the Dutch Reformed church. I went into the bathroom, a whole ten feet from her bed. Her tooth glass was empty, and the sink had drops of water on it. I filled the blue thumbprint tumbler, which according to her was Colonial, of course.

"Thank you, Young Allen." I made as if she was too weak to hold it herself, holding it right to her lips, and she shot her hand out and snatched it. "Thank you, I'm not that sick." And she bunched the white eyebrows into a major frown.

"Miss Claude, you don't look sick at all, you look especially nice today with your hair already combed, and your teeth in, too. That kidney must have kicked in just before I got here. Do I see you have your slippers on under the sheet?" My real job is to sort of keep her on her toes, see. (Joke, again.) Going all mournful wouldn't be any help.

Right away she said, "My feet were cold. Poor circulation, I've told you. Not that I expect your sympathy, of course. Step out while I dress myself, please." She handed me the glass and pulled her hand back under the spread and pressed at her side, frowning up at the far corner of the ceiling as if she were in too much pain to remember I was in the room. So I walked out.

She took two minutes max because as I expected under the covers she already had everything on. I didn't mind, though. I was glad it wasn't one of her really bad days like the week before, nothing but moaning and then we don't go out, just sit there. And I have to read to her, can you believe she doesn't like TV?

Today was the first break in a week of rainy days, too nice to sit inside even if you're paid for it. At least go across to the park, if she couldn't do more than that. Forget checking on that empty church, forget stopping for her caramels. Just sit, relax, and speculate about everyone else in the park. Get a lecture about her ancestors.

I opened the front door, watching the street. No kids — not that I cared. My foot started tapping even though it was only two minutes until the parlor doorknob squeaked and there she was, little gold earrings screwed on and hair all tucked up, reaching for my good arm.

"Hungry for sunshine, bright boy?" Stick in hand, little net bag over her wrist. "What're you waiting for?"

"For a certain old lady to get done with her makeup," I said right away. If I'd said, Nothing, Ma'am, she'd have been disappointed. She had a fresh dash of pink stuff on each cheek. Could've done it better with one of those magnified makeup mirrors, but I've checked and they're way expensive. She's old, anyhow. If she has no idea, what's the difference? I'm the only one who visits Miss Claude, me and that old retired last minister of the dead church, she's even older than him. My mom stops by on her lunch hour, when she can. "Are we going or not?" I managed to say it before she got her stick onto the doorstep. She pursed her mouth and jerked me out the door.

Locking her door is complicated, not just because of the three locks. If she keeps holding onto me she has to do the locking herself because of me having only the one good arm. If I let her go so I can lock it she has to find a good spot for her stick and get her other hand on the wall. I looked at her, because it makes no difference to me. Either she'd want to prove how tired she was today, or she'd want to show she was plenty strong enough to stand alone.

❊ ❊ ❊

It was a hard choice for her. Finally she said, "You do it. If you had two good arms it wouldn't be such a production, sir." Nothing stops Miss Claude, I'm telling you. She thumped her stick between some bricks—it's a brick walk—and placed two fingers against the door frame, like she was holding up the house.

"If I had two good arms I'd be playing football, not babysitting you," I told her. Which I think is true. I pulled her keyring out of my back pocket, careful not to pull my five out with it, and turned the locks, one two three, no problem. Seems I was meant to be left-handed, which is lucky, since my right arm got totally screwed when the doctor was yanking me out. We never sued because it was Mary Immaculate Hospital and my mother is a good Catholic unlike my Dutch Reformed father's family. So, zero money for me because a good Catholic does not sue Mary Immaculate, period. My Dad said it was lousy medical care, period, and they fought a lot about it before he split. We coulda had millions, yadda yadda.

So, not having millions, I continue to earn my four bucks an hour by politely offering Miss Claude my good arm and escorting her down the mossy old walk and out to the curb. The park is right across the street, four blocks square, and on a clear fall day like that one it is a fine place to hang out no matter how poor the neighborhood gets, sitting on a bench in the sunshine with acorns falling around your head and listening to an old lady tell stories.

We walked straight out to the curb; it took a few minutes because she actually does have a bum foot. Born wrong, like me. She has a special shoe when she goes out but still it doesn't point straight, and even with the extra two inches of built-up sole she walks funny. She hates how slow it makes her these days. I stopped and surveyed the traffic, easy since all the streets around here are one-way.

"We're jaywalking again, I see."

"Sorry, Miss Claude. I didn't realize you wanted to walk to the corner, stand there waiting for the light, and cross on the green with some baby carriage bumping us or a dog on a leash to trip you, and then walk all the way back to your favorite bench right across there. My mistake, let's go."

"Too late. All this standing on the curb, I'm already tired. Cross us and get it over with." She bent forward and put her stick down on the street, taking me with her. "At least you have two good eyes, that's a help. You are paying attention to the traffic, aren't you?"

We tottered across and up; she'll keep going as long as she needs to, over to her bench. "The usual, Ma'am? Or something exotic, perhaps the next bench? Or cross over that way, the one by those Indian ladies?"

"Oh, I think this will do. Perhaps they'll pass us by later." She made a small hiss, like something pneumatic sitting down, "Perhaps they'll circle the park to look at the old gal with the handsome escort." She looked at me with that twinkle she knows how to shine at you. Pleased with herself, for bothering to get out of the house at all. And maybe, thanking me for helping. And she was right, seems like women do check me out these days. Even smile, sometimes, but then, like all my life, whether they're Asian or Hispanic or European or whatever, when they see the arm, they'll look away. Do the pretending thing, I'm not here and they're not there and no one has seen anything, and that's that. I'm to the point where I don't even think about it. Like the kids in my high school, ignoring me because I'm not a jock. Or in a gang. I mean, what gang would want me?

At least the old lady can talk about it, doesn't act as if there's something terrible we can't mention. I stuck out my legs, settled back and closed my eyes, ready for an hour of nonstop lies about the old days. Sometimes she has to hand out helpful advice, I should do one-armed pushups, start an after-school computer club. Rah rah stuff she never does either. "Interrupt yourself if you see anyone good-looking coming this way," I told her.

I could have pulled out my Walkman, but she hates that, and anyhow I've heard every track I own a thousand times so I watched the kids playing in the leaves and the dogs running away from the cops and I let Miss Claude ramble on about her Sacred Ancestor, Rufus King. This park was named after him. She's not lying, I looked him up in the library. He did sign the Declaration of Independence, another true thing. And he died on his farm in guess where, right here. Jamaica, Queens. So this park is all that's left of acres of cows and sheep and corn and who knows what. Apple trees. Horses? His big white house is right in the middle, it's a museum now. Of course when I'm here it's never open. I could ask her sometime when it is, but that would encourage her. They say he was against slavery, it would be neat if that house was an Underground Railroad stop. But when she starts with how her ancestors owned land from here to Boston, and the Civil War general in the State of Washington and who followed who and who stole it or how they frittered it away I tune out. My mom says her family hasn't had real money since 1929.

So now sixty-five years later it's 1994 and I'm looking over at her house, all peeling, and noticing how sad it's gotten, with the roof all moldy and the turret tipping, about to slide. Thinking, if I had two good arms I could at least put in the glass, and meanwhile she was going on about the old Rufus King estate up in Massachusetts so I sat up and looked around and saw a little Spanish kid playing with his grandmother in a big drift of maple leaves and I poked Miss C in the ribs and pointed at them.

"Want to play in the leaves with me, Grandma?" We don't have to explain ourselves. And we never apologize; she doesn't so why should I?

Every time the kid would jump into the leaves he'd bury his face and the grandma would clap her hands and shout *"¿Hola? ¿Hola?"* The kid would laugh hysterically.

They were maybe fifty feet off, in a pile of leaves blown up against the spiked iron fence. "You're way too big for that little heap of leaves. Or are you expecting me to jump in and hide myself? Humph." And she thumped her stick at her own joke.

I grinned too, that was the whole idea. It was a good moment, people strolling and kids playing in the sunshine and nothing bad happening, why get upset about an old house turning into a wreck? Jamaica, Queens, is now crossroads to the world. West Indians and Asian Indians, African Americans and American Africans, Spanish people from South America and Europeans from Spain and Italy, even a couple of gimps descended from the English. All of us out for a nice day in the park, and so far so good. That's when I noticed someone else.

All right, it was this really pretty girl about my age walking along the path and going to pass our bench in a minute. She had thick black hair and eyebrows and big dark eyes and I think when I spotted her she looked away, quick. Over at the grandma and the little boy. But then she laughed out loud at the kid spraying leaves in the air so maybe she hadn't noticed me.

I kept smiling anyway hoping she would look back, and even if she didn't, she really was pretty and not at all city-girl tough looking. Just before she got to us, lo and behold she saw me and smiled back. I was on Miss C's left side so my good arm was stuck out along the back of the bench, my little arm was sort of up against Miss Claude, behind the sleeve of her coat. There was a chance the girl wouldn't notice anything. Which she didn't I winked and she just sort of laughed and smiled as she walked.

"*¡Hola!*"

That was not me. It was Miss Claude herself. Seemed she had noticed something, and decided to cause trouble. I didn't even think she could talk Spanish. I almost jumped in my seat, I would never have said anything first. But the girl stopped.

"*Hola, señora,*" she said. Just like that. I guess it's okay when an old person says something. "Nice day, isn't it?"

"Very nice, *signorina*. Or is that Italian?"

"It is *señorita*, in *Español, señora.*"

"And it's a nice day in English," I said. "*Señorita.*" And I smiled some more, but I didn't move. No point getting in her face and all. She nodded and seemed to be hesitating so I asked, "Know them?" I waved over at the grandmother and kid. With my left hand.

"Yes. That's my grandmother. And my little cousin."

I was glad it wasn't her kid. People have been leaving my school pregnant every year since eighth grade. The action some guys get never fails to amaze me. I didn't know her, so I figured she must go to the Catholic school. They're supposed to keep a tighter lid on the students. Maybe. "You going to jump in the leaves too?"

That made her giggle. "His mother wants him back, I came to tell Grandma." She made a face. "She won't like it. I have to get them both to go home now."

"Let them have their fun, dear. Sit down by us for a minute, and tell us your name?"

I nearly fell off the bench but Miss C looked like absolutely nothing was happening. And the girl sat. She settled on the other end of the bench from me, sort of balanced on the front part. Like not exactly nervous, but looking over at the fence and back.

"My name is Sondra." She nodded and waited, serious.

"My name is Claude. You may call me Miss Claude. And this is Young Allen."

"Miss Claude. Allen. Very nice to meet you. Are you also the grandmother and her grandson?"

Before I could answer Miss C said, "No. He's not my grandson. I have never married, my dear. Therefore I have no progeny, unlike today's movie stars and young people." She patted the back of her hair, touching at the big tortoise shell pins she sticks it up with. "Young Allen is my date."

"What!" We both shouted it, then we looked at each other and laughed.

Miss Claude looked smug. "It's my charm, Sondra." And she twinkled at the girl, who smiled back. Miss C was looking pretty cute for an interfering old lady, but Sondra was beautiful. She even had perfect teeth, and probably not from orthodonture.

"Your charm?" I gave the old lady the evil look I've used since my savage kindergarten days. "Any woman who wants can date me, for four dollars an hour."

Sondra looked confused, but the old lady thumped her stick and nodded. "Yes, yes. And worth it at twice the price."

"Really?" I said, and I raised my eyebrows. "I could use it, Grandma." Now Sondra really looked confused.

"I haven't got it, don't get any ideas," Miss Claude snapped. "You make me tired. All this fresh air and sunshine makes me tired. Why don't the two of you go over and bother that other grandmother?" And she put her hands together on top of her stick and made to lean her head forward and close her eyes. "Give Sondra a hand with retrieving her cousin, Young Allen. Let me alone, I want my *siesta* now."

Sondra looked at me, like she was okay with that, but not me. I was annoyed. I knew what the old witch was up to, it had to be obvious to Sondra too even if she did think it was a fine idea. But a girl like that would have a boyfriend already. And what was the point? A casual chat with her on the bench like everything was normal, that was plenty for me. That was a lot. Sondra saw me frowning and got up right away, now we were both embarrassing her. I was sorry but it still didn't make me want to stand up in front of her. The old lady opened her left eye and peered at me, next thing she'd be pushing me off with her stick.

"Miss Claude, I'm supposed take care of you until I get you back home." I kept my voice easy, like nothing was happening. "If some jerk comes along and does something while I'm over there, my mother'll kill me."

"*Buenos dias.*" I was almost relieved when Sondra turned toward the path but Miss Claude was quick, wide awake in a second and grabbing her wrist.

"Wait, Sondra dear. It's not you." She whipped back her coat sleeve and there was the old right arm, in all its tiny puppet glory.

"He didn't want to scare you. He doesn't mind talking about it, if you don't."

Which I realized was generally true. Mostly. But she had spoiled my nice little personal moment, making some kind of truth-in-packaging statement, and I did mind. I was ready to leave the both of them and head for home, for the privacy of my own room at the top of a ten-story building. Close the door and boot up the old computer. No employers, no pretty strangers pretending my right arm didn't exist. It was only four-thirty, no Mom around asking questions.

When guys gang up on you, you're better off not running. If you have to, a swift kick where it hurts. Taking off is a final option. But this time the interfering hag had gone too far. Let her get herself home. Let her new best friend Sondra get her home. I shook myself to my feet and prepared to stalk away.

"Young Allen?" Sondra was looking straight at the arm. Right at the freaky little thing, and I realized, she could see it. Unlike everybody else on the planet. So, I waited. "That's a birth injury, right? The *herida*, your arm. What do you call it in English?"

"My arm? I call it Arthur. Hah, hah. Sorry." Stupid, obscure reference to a sixties rock group. Actually, to myself I call it Buddy. "It's an Erb's palsy. And yeah, it's a birth thing. These days you don't see them, they cut the kid out."

"With a good doctor it doesn't have to happen." She sounded almost angry. "You should have been paid a lot of money for unnecessary and permanent damage. I am going to become a lawyer and I intend to help people who are wrongly injured."

"Don't get yourself all in knots about it," I said. "It's my problem."

"You have been hurt and should be compensated. Because of that Erb's you can't play sports, right? Drive a car? Even a bike."

Actually she was right about the car, which was one big reason why we didn't move out to the burbs with all the extended cousins. Buses and subways needed for the one-armed bandit. That, and my mother's good job. In the Jamaica Courthouse, over twenty years now. "So what? I can run fine, faster than most. I could play tennis if I wanted. I surf the net, I'm the best one-handed gamester on the Web." I stopped myself, what did she care?

"Oh, on the Web? Young Allen, the one-armed Spiderman?"

"Good girl, Sondra." Miss Claude cackled and did her thing again with the stick. I guess she liked the way her game was playing out. "You have backbone, and brains too."

"Thank you. I also have—never mind. I must go and persuade my grandmother now. It was a pleasure to meet both of you." She shook Miss Claude's hand, looked at me and back at the fence.

I looked at Miss Claude, who nodded her head about five times, so I gave in. "All right, all right. I'll come along and evaluate your powers of advocacy."

"Advocacy, like *un abogado*?"

"Right. If you can talk your grandmother into leaving I might hire you." We started walking.

"Sorry, Young Allen, but you are too old already. For the law, I mean. Ten years old is even too old. Unless you're a really, really mature nine-year-old?" She looked at me demurely. I laughed and told her I was a really, really mature sixteen, and she laughed, too. Then she sighed. "I'm fifteen and it feels like forever until I can go to law school. Did you ever try to make the doctor compensate you?"

So I explained about my mom the good Catholic. "You're a Catholic? You seem like one of those George Washington types."

"That's my father. His family all went to that empty old church up the block. He lives in Canada." I haven't seen old Dad in years, I just wanted to make it clear I knew who he was.

"That's a creepy place." She shuddered. "Those blank windows, and all dark inside." I mostly think it's just sad, with the stained glass sold and gone, but I could see her point and I was agreeing with her as we reached Grandma and the kid.

The grandmother was tiny, and all bent over looking at the boy who was now on his back, swishing his arms and legs like he thought he could make a leaf angel. We stood and watched until they noticed us. Right away the old woman took her hands off her knees and straightened up a little, but not much, frowning.

"*¿Que hora es?*" She looked at me and back down at her grandson right away, like we should both go away.

"I told you she wouldn't want to see me." Sondra was talking behind her hand. "She won't believe me the time's really up."

"I got that." I understand a little Spanish, you'd better if you grow up in Jamaica, Queens. Of course if it's Cuban, that makes it more interesting. "She speak any English?"

"A little. But she understands, more than she lets on. Let's go, Roberto. Mami's waiting!" Sondra was smiling, holding out her hands to the boy.

The old lady turned to me. "*¿Ya es hora para irnos?*" Looking very suspicious. Clearly she didn't want to believe Sondra. I didn't say anything, just showed her my watch, on the good arm, and smiled as she peered at the dial and up at me, shaking her head like it was a conspiracy. Then her face changed. She'd noticed my other arm. She turned her head away like it was bad luck to see a withered arm or something, and spat. "*¡Inocente!*" She hissed, and grabbed the little kid by the hand. She pulled him up and started hobbling like crazy down the path.

"*¡Abuelita!*" Sondra gasped and looked at me, clasping her hands, but I shrugged. By now nothing bothers me, even an old Cuban lady who thinks an Erb's palsy means a person is simple-minded. Some people actually think you can give them cripple cooties. If she was afraid for her precious grandson I could only feel sorry for her.

They were almost at Miss C's bench, so I just said, "Let 'em go, we can follow them. They go home, you don't have to do anything." I joked about it. "She's right, I am innocent."

"But I am so sorry, Allen." Sondra was trying to smile back but embarrassment was winning out. "She's always that way, but—not this bad. Sometimes I think she's crazy."

"Maybe, but look at the bright side. Your old bat's making great time, almost up to my old lady." Which is where we caught them.

Sondra ran right around in front of them and stopped her grandmother. "*¡Grand-mami! Por favor, esperate.*" She took a deep breath and said, "Miss Claude, may I present to you my Grandma Señora Eloisa Maria Lugo. *Abuelita*, Miss Claude. She is our neighbor."

Señora Eloisa tossed a quick nod at Miss C and then whispered to Sondra, good and loud as if Miss C and I were too deaf to hear. "*¡Tres brazos y cinco piernas!*"

I had to laugh. "Three arms and five legs, Miss Claude. That just about described you and me, doesn't it?" By this time Sondra had tears in her eyes. I shook my head, no problem.

Except the little kid started jumping around pointing, "Five legs! Five legs!" He got that out about two-and-a-half times and then Sondra slapped her hand over his mouth and held on while he jerked and twisted like a madman.

"Madame, your manners disgrace your family." Miss Claude was suddenly teetering to her feet and thumping her stick on the ground in front of the little spitfire. "These two young people put you to shame."

"Sondra! We have no time for this—*no tengo tiempo para un tullido que no puede cuidarse*!" Señora Eloisa faced Miss Claude. "*O usted*, old woman!" she snapped. Miss Claude just looked blank, and I didn't get all of it, myself. I wanted to let it ride, let Señora Grandma get the heck out of the park and on home.

But not Sondra. "They are my friends!" Now she was mad, too. "How can you say that?" She lost her grip on the kid and he dived under the bench and balled himself up. Grandma opened her mouth but Miss Claude got in there first.

"You old fool! It's his arm, isn't it? He has a withered arm, is that a mortal sin? Do you realize this Young Allen is a straight-A student at Jamaica High School, and his mother runs Judge

Jenkins' whole courtroom? He has a brilliant future, not to mention a family going back practically as far as mine, you, you—you
immigrant!"

That was nasty. I tried to put my arm around my old lady,
steer her away before one of them had a stroke or something. She
shook me off.

Grand-mami was just getting warmed up. "Immigrant! *Con
su permiso, no para nada vivria* to this America *esta muerta la imitad del
ano!*" Now her back was straight as a ramrod, and she was shriek-
ing up at Miss Claude, who was looking completely blank. "I
would no have abandoned my home if—*si no fuera par mi hijo y ese
carajo de revolucion.*"

"The revolution? *¡Aqui no hay ninguna revolucion, abuelita!* This
is fifty years ago." Sondra again.

"The Revolution! How dare you talk about the Revolution!"
Miss C trumpeted. That word, she understood. "My ancestor
fought in that bloody war. To make this a free country for anybody, even the likes of you, to come and live a good life. Safe,
prosperous and free."

"Please, no, please! Miss Claude, she is a little crazy. Please
understand, she had to leave Cuba because of Castro. Leave her
whole life behind. Her oldest son was killed, my Mami says she is
never the same. My uncle was—handicapped," she finished softly.

"Well, that's irrelevant now," snorted Miss Claude. "In
America it's your brain that counts. This boy is a computer ge-
nius," and she darted a quick look at me, like, keep still. "Don't
you go yet, young man. Time's not up." Screaming fights I do not
need; I was absolutely ready to leave them to it.

"*Es muy bueno con las compus,*" Sondra announced, pointing
at me. Like, me being good at computers was supposed to mean
something to Grand-mami?

"Take my email?" I said quickly, smiling. I was hoping she'd
laugh, break it up, but no, she took a breath and started in again on
Señora Eloisa.

"His grand—his friend Miss Claude, she says in America, *la
mente y no los musculos*—"

"*Es muy bueno con las compus,* Sondra," Grand-mami said right
back. Making sure Miss Claude knew Sondra was as good on the
computer as me. That did surprise me. "*El ni siquera pode hablar por
simismo.*" And she sniffed.

That did it. "Talk for myself!" I shouted. "*¿Con tres damas ya hablando deja, señora?* And not even listening to each other?" I threw up both arms, and the fingers on the little one flapped at Grandma. "Listen, Miss Claude. She's asking why I don't defend myself? With three women talking already at the same time!" I glared at the three of them standing there with their mouths open. "Just don't all you three start in on me now." I was sure I was as good as finished with Sondra after that but to my amazement she started laughing and even Grandma cackled once, by God. Miss C smiled serenely.

"Young Allen, perhaps living here in Jamaica you are becoming more Latin than you think." Sondra was holding out her right hand. I looked at her. What, was she some kind of freak freak? She put her left hand on her hip, kept her right hand stuck out there. "You have a right hand, sir. I don't think anyone has cut it off."

So I stepped up and got the floppy hand under her hand, then I bent over quick and kissed the back of hers. Thinking, well, you asked, how do you like it?

Sondra laughed, a pleased sounding laugh. "*Es un caballero de España, abuelita.*"

"*Mas o menos. Su Castillano es muy malo.*"

"Now my Spanish is no good? " I pulled out my notepad, and smiled. "Good as your English." I scribbled something and handed the page to Sondra. "My email, Señorita Abogada. Do you have a card?"

"Not yet, smart guy." But she slipped it into her jeans pocket and now she put both hands on her hips. "*¡A casa, abuelita! ¡A mami, muchacho!*"

So they walked away, and I watched her a couple of minutes, thinking, nice. Everything in the right place, when there was a sound beside me. I hadn't noticed, Miss Claude was sitting down again, and she was looking funny.

"Miss C? Miss Claude?" She was almost blue. I thought fast. "Miss Claude, I'm calling 911." She was breathing, but barely, I wished to hell I knew CPR, there must be CPR for one-armed people, because how about in wars? "Hold on, I'm calling." I just got my mobile open when she whispered something. I leaned over and thought I heard, "Wait." It came again, like distant wind. "Just wait."

"Fuck waiting! You're going blue!" I felt her cheek. "And cold!"

She made a sound, I had to lean in. Sounded like, "Language, young . . . man." Correcting my manners with her dying breath?

"Shut up!" I shouted. "Shut up while I talk!" She jumped, and her eyes cracked a gleam.

It was right in her ear, I guess I blasted the old brain. I whispered, "Sorry, Miss C, but let me call." Next thing I knew her withered fingers were creeping around my phone and she was whispering some more. I put my ear to her mouth

"The excitement. Too much. I need. Rest." She drew out the last word, made it sound so peaceful, and final.

"Miss Claude." It's hard to whisper when you're desperate. "You need oxygen, or a shot, or something. You could die."

She started making a funny little *oh, oh, oh* noise and unbelievably, I realized, she was laughing. Laughing. When she stopped the blue was gone from around her mouth, there was even pink in her lips. "Dance on my grave, if you dare." She whispered it, and then she laughed that laugh again, only it finished in a little tinkle.

I was up so close I was practically breathing down her throat, her face gone all blurry like your fingers do when you spread out your hand flat against your nose and suddenly I saw shining up at me the biggest, bluest, widest eyes, as deep as any girl's I ever saw, and I just froze, bent over, feeling for an endless moment everything some old beau must've felt about eighty years ago, when he gathered up his courage to move in and she gave him the treatment. I couldn't speak, I just stared without breathing, believing in my body the warm, serious, delicious promises I have never ever allowed myself to hope for in my life, until finally she squeezed my hand and shut her eyes tight so I saw all the wrinkles around them and then she let go. She patted my cheek softly and covered her mouth and did it again, almost too quiet to hear: *oh, oh, oh.*

I sat up right away and for a second I thought I was going to puke. A hard-on for a hundred-year-old lady? Whoa, gross. Way too disgusting to tell anyone. Never, ever, not even a priest, if I did ever go to Mom's church again. I was definitely the crazy one in this park today. Señora Eloisa was right, I must be an idiot. As far as I was concerned, if Miss C didn't want 911 she should just go home now, as fast as possible. Time was definitely up for me.

I was still shaking my head, sweating, when I heard her clear her throat. She was sitting straight up, like nothing had happened.

"Not planning to die until I've taught you a few things, Young Allen." She thumped her stick. I jumped, but she waved her hand, don't worry. "Now that you're finally growing up. Yes, I know you're six feet, and probably more to go, but what do you know about women?"

The silence was embarrassing. God, was she going to start in on the birds and the bees?

She smoothed her hair again and laughed. "Just a few airs and graces, my dear. How do they put it? Information to your advantage." She looked off into the late afternoon sunshine, I suppose remembering.

"Okay, Miss Claude. So if you know so much how come you never got married?"

"Spanish flu took the only man I didn't think was sorry for me, or after my money." I nodded, I got it. She nodded back. "Of course. You'd rather be alone." The stick thumped again but this time I didn't bother to jump. Of course she could read my mind.

"Get me home now, dear boy, I need my bed." She took my good arm, and I helped her up. "Next week, we'll talk." We started the shuffle to the street but then she stopped and put both her hands on the stick. "Hiding in your room and emailing a lovely young woman is not a life, sir." The old eyebrows were doing their bunching thing. "I know what I say."

"Oh, yeah?" I was thinking, what're you talking about? Butt out, lady, your creepy solitary life in your falling-down house has nothing to do with me. I stared at her and she stared right back until I finally saw, like, oh yes. You do know.

I put little Buddy across my chest and bowed. Then I gave her my good arm and I helped her to the other side of the street and up to her door, both of us pretty quiet.

I put her to bed, and I didn't tell her, but the whole time my mind was running on Sondra. I decided that was all right, though.

Garden

In the ruined garden it is my mother
I grieve for, her attempt year after year
to keep order, to keep up appearances. I spent
wet green summers weeding our narrow yard
after breakfast, before the noon heat struck, while
my mother hung out the wash, out of sight.
Squatting among her morning glories and nasturtium,
I pulled up what had sprouted overnight, their roots
fragrant with evening rain. I gathered in my hands
what was unwanted and wild, learning to distinguish
what to love, to discard. Working on my knees
around the carefully arranged boulders growing
soft, dark moss would teach me discipline,
to know what endures. Yet by mid-August
I couldn't keep up with the daily crop of weeds,
and my mother gave in each summer
in silence. Now in my own garden
nothing I plant takes hold, only this
unasked-for bounty of weeds. Each evening
I take in this bitter harvest, this weeding out of
what is too unruly for me, this knowing that
that it will be there again tomorrow, regardless.

Rearrangement of the Invisible

And here he comes again, that querulous old man
with his pointy hat, his knobby walking-stick,
curl-toed shoes, pulling behind him the next installment
of your life, whether you're ready or not,
sweeping ahead in his pushbroom the scraps
and shards of your story so far—

Just as you were getting used to the white roses,
those blowsy blooms along the edges of the lawn,
the doe steps delicately out of the dark
while you're sleeping, incises every bud,
every blossom, leaving naked sticks piercing
the night, and despite the dog throwing herself
against the door, by the time you push it open,
stagger out in your threadbare nightshirt,
the deer has slipped away like a ghost
into the woods beyond the pointless fence.

You wake in the morning to a whole new landscape,
and when you cry out, wringing your hands and cursing,
the dog sits down and fixes you in her patient gaze—
she tried to tell you (but you wouldn't wake up)
that the old man was passing down the road
rearranging your future, and the thing growing
in your bones, which won't be identified for weeks,
is the seed of a whole new order.

Something Coming

We are beginning to understand something
of what is coming, to go beyond sensing a shadow
in the woods watching us, and to see it take shape,
see it coming toward us across a field, zigzagging
as it does, now standing idle and watching the sky,
now heading directly for us at a trot. And realizing
that we are seen, that it will find us no matter
what we do, we are slowing down.
                                                    We are
standing very still hoping to blend with the waving
greens of this raw springtime, to stay upwind
of it as warmer breezes pick up and buffet the leaves,
the grasses, tossing everything in a moving salad
of life; we sway on our legs, trying to move with the air
that surrounds us, and we stop thinking of what is around
the next bend in the path, stop planning our next
escape route, and begin to merge with the moment;
we have slipped into a painting by Van Gogh;
something is coming again across the fields and we
are open as sunflowers in full bloom
to these last moments on the earth.

Martha Kennedy, *Windblown Sunflowers*, oil on panel, 38" x 54"

DIANA ANHALT has received four *ByLine Magazine* poetry prizes, was an *Ekphrasis* Chapbook Contest finalist, and was awarded the Rabino Jacobo Goldberg prize for non-fiction. Her poetry has appeared in *The Comstock Review*, *The Litchfield Review*, *Clare Literary Journal*, *Buckle &*, *The Scholar & Feminist*, and *DayBreak*, and elsewhere. She is the author of a chapbook, *Shiny Objects*, and of *A Gathering of Fugitives: American Political Expatriates in Mexico 1948-1965*.

SULTANA BANULESCU is a Ph.D. Candidate at the City University of New York Graduate Center and the 2010-2011 recipient of the Randolph Braham Dissertation Fellowship in Eastern European History and Holocaust Studies. Her short story, *Beggars and Thieves*, a coming-of-age tale set in Bucharest's formerly Jewish neighborhood, is centered upon the historical events of March 4, 1977, that claimed 1,570 lives and almost 33,000 buildings.

SHASHI BHAT is an assistant professor of creative writing at Dalhousie University in Halifax, Canada. She received her M.F.A. in fiction from The Johns Hopkins University, has published stories in several journals, including *The Threepenny Review* and *The Missouri Review*, and was nominated for a Pushcart Prize. Her first novel is forthcoming from Cormorant Books in 2012.

AURORA BRACKETT likes to swim and often fantasizes about having gills. Her poems and stories have been published in *TinFish*, *The Portland Review*, *Cosmopsis*, and other literary magazines. She lives in Oakland, California.

GLADYS JUSTIN CARR is a former Nicholson Fellow at Smith University, a University Fellow at Cornell University, and a publishing excutive with McGraw-Hill and HarperCollins book publishers. Her work has appeared in numerous publications, including *The New York Times*, *North Atlantic Review*, and *The South Carolina Review*. She is the author of *Augustine's Brain — The Remix* and a forthcoming chapbook, *A Premise of Blue*.

MAXINE CHERNOFF is a professor and Chair of the Creative Writing program at San Francisco State University. She edits the long-running literary journal *New American Writing*. She is the author of six books of fiction and nine books of poetry, including her most recent, *The Turning*. With Paul Hoover, she has translated *The Selected Poems of Friedrich Hölderlin*, which won the PEN USA 2009 Translation Award.

JUDITH HUTCHINSON CLARK received her M.A. in Nineteenth-Century Literature and her M.F.A. in Creative Writing from Sarah Lawrence College. She has published three short story collections, including a novel in stories. Her story in this issue, "Girlfriend," reflects her love for Hawaii, where she spent her first ten years. Jamaica, Queens, New York, is, like Honolulu, an open door to the rest of the world.

SUZANNE CLEARY's poetry books are *Keeping Time* (2002) and *Trick Pear* (2007), both published by Carnegie Mellon. Recipient of a Pushcart Prize, her poems have appeared in *The Atlantic Monthly, Ploughshares, Poetry London,* and the anthology *Best American Poetry.* She holds an M.A. in Writing from Washington University and a Ph.D. in Literature and Criticism from Indiana University of Pennsylvania. She is Professor of English at SUNY Rockland.

GAIL RUDD ENTREKIN has taught poetry and English literature at California colleges for 25 years. Her most recent collection of poems, *Change (Will Do You Good)* (Poetic Matrix Press), was nominated for a Northern California Book Award. She is editor of the online environmental literary journal *Canary* and Poetry Editor of Hip Pocket Press.

BARBARA A. FISCHER's short stories have appeared in *CALYX, Tampa Review, Sycamore Review, The MacGuffin, Wind,* and *Nimrod,* among other journals. She lives and writes in Versailles, Kentucky, and is a recipient of the Kentucky Arts Council's Al Smith Fellowship.

MADELYN GARNER is a retired public school administrator in Denver, Colorado. Her work has appeared in many literary journals, including *Water-Stone Review, PMS poemmemoirstory, Saranac Review, Bryant Literary Review, Margie,* and *Harpur Palate,* as well as in the anthology *Beyond Forgetting: Poetry and Prose about Alzheimer's Disease.* She is a past recipient of the Colorado Governor's Award for Excellence in the Arts and Humanities.

MICHAEL GARRIGA, a graduate of Florida State University's Ph.D. program in creative writing, lives in Tallahassee, where he teaches full time. "Fiesta de Semana Santa" is a part of his forthcoming book, *Duels* (Milkweed Editions). Other duels have been published in, or accepted by, *The Southern Review, New Letters, story South, Black Warrior Review, Surreal South '09,* and elsewhere.

JOELL HALLOWELL is an experimental filmmaker and writer in San Francisco. She has recently collected video oral histories from which she co-edited *Take Me to the River: Fishing, Swimming, and Dreaming on the San Joaquin* (Heyday Books, 2010). She was an assistant editor and interviewer for *Underground America* (McSweeney's 2009) and is currently compiling an oral history and photography book in collaboration with author Nona Caspers, *Here Came the Brides.*

TOM HANSEN is a retired teacher living in the Black Hills of South Dakota. His poems have appeared in *The American Scholar, The Literary Review, The Midwest Quarterly, Poetry Northwest, Southern Poetry Review,* and elsewhere. His first book of poetry, *Falling to Earth,* was awarded the A. Poulin, Jr., Poetry Prize and published by BOA Editions in 2006.

JEFF HARDIN teaches at Columbia State Community College and lives in Tennessee. His work appears most recently in *The Southern Review, Southwest Review, The Hudson Review, Hotel Amerika, Poetry Northwest, Tar River Poetry,* and elsewhere. He is the author of two chapbooks and one collection, *Fall Sanctuary,* recipient of the Nicholas Roerich Prize.

NICOLE HARDY is the author of the poetry collections *This Blonde* and *Mud Flap Girl's XX Guide to Facial Profiling,* which was published as part of *Main Street Rag*'s 2006 Editor's Choice chapbook series. One of her essays was recently featured in the *New York Times* "Modern Love" column, and she has poems forthcoming in *Sanskrit Literary Arts Magazine* and *Ellipsis.*

PATRICIA HAWLEY is a recent first-place winner of The 25th Tennessee Williams Literary Festival 2011 Poetry Prize, where four of her poems were selected for the Louisiana Humanities Institute literary journal, *Louisiana Cultural Vistas.* Her work has appeared in numerous other publications, including the anthology *Into The Open.* She enjoys painting, acting, and being with her large family.

JOSH KALSCHEUR's poems have appeared in or are forthcoming from *Boston Review, Witness,* and *The Cincinnati Review,* among others. Recently nominated for a Pushcart Prize, he currently resides in Madison, Wisconsin, where he is a poetry editor for *Devil's Lake.*

CAITLIN KINDERVATTER-CLARK is a Henry Hoyns/Poe-Faulkner fellow in the M.F.A. program at the University of Virginia, where she teaches creative and academic writing. She grew up in Washington, D.C. This is her first publication.

KATIE KINGSTON is the author of three poetry collections: *In My Dreams Neruda, El Rio de las Animas Perdidas,* and *Unwritten Letters.* Her poems have appeared in *Atlanta Review, Hawai'i Review, Hunger Mountain, Margie, Nimrod, The Pinch, RUNES,* and *Sugar House Review.* Her translations have appeared in *Nimrod International Journal: Mexico/USA* and in *Mexican Poetry Today: 20/20 Voices,* Shearsman Books, UK.

SUSANNA KITTREDGE is a Massachusetts native who earned her M.F.A. in Creative Writing from San Francisco State University. Her work has appeared in the journals *Sahara, Shampoo, Sidebrow, Parthenon West Review, 14 Hills,* and many others, as well as the Faux Press anthology *Bay Poetics.* She is currently an office manager and aspiring teacher.

CLARK KNOWLES teaches writing at the University of New Hampshire. He received his M.A. in fiction writing from the University of New Hampshire, and his M.F.A. in Writing from Bennington College. The Arts Council of the State of New Hampshire awarded him an Individual Fellowship for the year 2009. His fiction has appeared or is forthcoming in *Eclipse, PANK, Glimmer Train Stories, Zahir, The Inkwell Review, Red Rock Review, Black Warrior Review, Scribner's Best of Fiction Workshops,* and *Flying Horse Review.*

LINDSAY KNOWLTON is a past recipient of a fellowship from the Massachusetts Artists Foundation, funded by the Massachusetts Council for the Arts and Humanities. Her poems have appeared in *The Boston Review, CODA, Ploughshares, Indiana Review, Green Mountains Review, The Writer's Voice of the West Side Y,* and *The Spoon River Poetry Review.* Her first book, *Earthly Freight,* appeared in 2009.

RACHEL INEZ LANE is finishing the last year of her M.F.A. at Florida State University. Her writing has been in the *Orlando Sentinel, Los Angeles Times, Boxcar Poetry Review, LA Review,* and *Rattle;* her poem, "To Whoever Wrote: MEEsha! MY dick n' YO Mouf!," was selected as the winner of the 2011 *Washington Square* Award for poetry. She is currently working on her first book of poetry, entitled *This Heart Goes Bang.*

GENNY LIM is a native San Francisco poet, playwright, performer and educator, who has been featured in poetry festivals throughout the U.S., Italy, Bosnia-Hercegovina and Latin America. She is the author of the award-winning play, *Paper Angels,* co-author of *Island: The Poetry and History of Chinese Immigrants on Angel Island,* and two collections of poetry.

PETER LUDWIN is the recipient of a Literary Fellowship from Artist Trust. His first book, *A Guest in All Your Houses,* was published in 2009 by Word Walker Press. His work has appeared in numerous journals, including *The Bitter Oleander, The Comstock Review,* and *The Warwick Review.* He has poems forthcoming in *The North American Review* and *Prairie Schooner.*

NATHAN MCCLAIN currently lives and works in Los Angeles. His poems have recently appeared or are forthcoming in *Columbia Poetry Review, Cave Wall, Water-Stone Review, DIAGRAM, Pebble Lake Review,* and *Best New Poets 2010.*

181

JAMES MEETZE's book *Dayglo* was selected by Terrance Hayes as winner of the 2010 Sawtooth Poetry Prize and published by Ahsahta Press. He is also the author of *I Have Designed This For You* (2007), and editor, with Simon Pettet, of *Other Flowers: Uncollected Poems by James Schuyler* (2010). He has taught poetry and creative writing at the University of California, San Diego, California State University, San Marcos, and in the M.F.A. Program at National University. He lives in San Diego with his wife and son.

MARY B. MOORE, a poet, teacher, and scholar, has published recently in *Cavalier Literary Couture, Connotations Press, 2River View, American Poetry Journal*, and *Prairie Schooner*. Her previous credits include *Field, Poetry, New Letters*, and *Nimrod*. Cleveland State University Poetry Center published her poetry collection, *The Book of Snow* (1997), and Southern Illinois University Press published the critical book, *Desiring Voices, Women Sonneteers and Petrarchism* (2000).

BRENT PALLAS lives in New York City as a freelance designer doing everything from making tables to creating owl bookends from socks. His work has been in *Poetry, The Southern Review, The New England Review, Verse Daily, 2River View, The Missouri Review* and other journals. He has been dominated for Pushcart Prizes and was a finalist for the 2007 Pablo Neruda Prize for Poetry.

LUCY RICCIARDI has been seriously studying and writing poetry for the last four years. Her poems range from formal sonnets to free verse, many dealing with past experiences. A retired CFO of Hyperion Software, she also likes to write poems about the nexus of religion and finance/accounting.

PAIGE RIEHL's prose and poetry have been published or are forthcoming in several publications, most recently *Blood Orange Review, Word Riot, Avatar Review*, and *Emprise Review*. A full-time college literature and writing teacher from St. Paul, Minnesota, she holds an M.A. in English from North Dakota State University, a B.S. in Mass Communications from Minnesota State University Moorhead, and is currently working toward an M.F.A. in Creative Writing from Hamline University.

ROBERT (RUSTY) RUSSELL is an economist and host/producer of the program *Radio Literature* on WORT-FM, Madison, Wisconsin. He has taught performance poetry workshops throughout the Midwest and at the Universidad Autonoma de Chihuahua, Mexico, for several years. He has a grown daughter, Callie, and he lives in Madison with his wife, Elizabeth Sedillo Russell.

HAYDEN SAUNIER's first book of poetry, *Tips for Domestic Travel*, was published last year by Black Lawrence Press. Her work has appeared in *Beloit Poetry Journal*, *Drunken Boat*, *Rattle*, *Nimrod*, and *U.S 1*, among other journals. She won the 2005 Robert Fraser Poetry Award and has been nominated twice for a Pushcart Prize.

STEPHEN TAYLOR teaches writing and mythology at Glendale College. He has won the L.A. Arts Council Literature Award, the 2004 *Main Street Rag* Short Fiction Contest, and has been and a two-time finalist in *Nimrod*'s Katherine Anne Porter Prize for Fiction. His story collection, *Cut Men*, was published by Main Street Rag in 2005. His story "The Great Awakening" is forthcoming in the anthology *The Book of Villains*, and he has co-edited a sports anthology, *Suicidally Beautiful*, both of which are to be published this fall.

KYOKO UCHIDA's poetry, prose, and translations have been published in *The Georgia Review*, *Grand Street*, *Manoa*, *New Letters*, *Prairie Schooner*, *The Virginia Quarterly Review*, and other journals, and anthologized in *Stories in the Stepmother Tongue* (White Pine Press, 2000) and *An Ear to the Ground* (Cune Press, 1997). Raised in Japan, the United States, and Canada, she holds an M.F.A. in poetry from Cornell University. Her poetry collection *Elsewhere* is forthcoming from Texas Tech University Press in 2012.

YOLANDA VALENZUELA was born in Santiago Papasquiaro, Durango, Mexico, and emigrated to California at the age of three. She teaches reading, composition, and literature at a community college in the San Francisco Bay Area.

MARK WAGENAAR the 2011 winner of the Felix Pollak Prize, for his book *Voodoo Inverso*. A graduate of the University of Virginia's M.F.A. program he will be transferring from the University of Utah's Ph.D. program to the University of North Texas. His poems have been accepted or published by a wide variety of magazines, including the *New England Review*, *Subtropics*, *The Southern Review*, *American Literary Review*, *Crab Orchard Review*, */nor*, *The Antioch Review*, *The South Carolina Review*, *The North American Review*, *Phoebe*, *Tar River Poetry*, and *Poetry East*.

ARNE WEINGART attended Dartmouth College, where he received a B.A. in German and Comparative Literature and studied poetry with Richard Eberhart, and Columbia University, where he received an M.F.A. in writing. More recently he was awarded a writing residency at the Atlantic Center for the Arts, working with Rosellen Brown. He and his family live in Chicago, where he is the owner and principal of a graphic design consultancy specializing in identity and wayfinding.

KELLIE WELLS is the author of the short story collection *Compression Scars*, winner of the Flannery O'Connor Prize, and the novel *Skin*. She teaches in the creative writing programs at the University of Alabama and Pacific University.

SARAH WETZEL is the author of *Bathsheba Transatlantic*, winner of The Philip Levine Prize for Poetry and published in November 2010. A Pushcart Prize nominee for 2009 and 2010, her work appears in U.S. and Israeli publications including *Barrow Street*, *Valparaiso*, *Quiddity*, *Rattle*, *Pedestal*, *Folly*, *TwoReview*, and others. She divides her time between Tel Aviv and Manhattan where she lives with a husband and one needy dog.

MEG WITHERS teaches English at Merced Community College, and is a committed community activist. In addition to her books *Must Be Present to Win* (Ghost Road Press, 2006) and *A Communion of Saints* (TinFish Press, 2008), her work has been anthologized and appears in journals and re views. She is currently working on two books, as well as a collaborative stage adaptation of her book, *A Communion of Saints*, a story of the AIDS epidemic in Hawaii during the 1980's.

CORRECTIONS

In our Spring/Summer 2011 issue, *Growing Season*, we mistakenly identified contributor Katrina Rutt as Katrine Rutt.

About the Artists

CONNIE BRYSON'S oil paintings have been displayed in Los Angeles and in national galleries, buildings, restaurants and spas. Her work being published by Winn Devon Art Group and can be seen throughout the United States and the world. She is represented by Joseph Gierek Fine Art in Tulsa, Oklahoma.

TODD CAMP is an artist represented by Joseph Gierek Fine Art in Tulsa, Oklahoma.

GLENN HERBERT DAVIS was the recipient of a Oklahoma Visual Arts Fellowship in 2006. His work has been exhibited and published nationally. His solo work, "image of one," was exhibited at Berry College.

MICHAEL DEROSA is an artist represented by Joseph Gierek Fine Art in Tulsa, Oklahoma.

KATHRYN DUNLEVIE'S work has been featured in *The New York Times*, the *San Francisco Chronicle*, the *San Jose Mercury News*, and *Artweek*, as well as internationally in *La Fotografia Actual*, *Art of England*, and *Profifoto*. Her work is shown internationally and has been included in exhibitions at Belgravia Gallery and Vertigo in London, Studio Thomas Kellner in Germany, as well as at Washington, D.C.'s Art Museum of the Americas, Michael Mazzeo Gallery in New York, and other venues.

MARTHA KENNEDY is a Santa Fe-based artist whose art has been exhibited in numerous solo and group exhibitions. She is represented in Tulsa by Joseph Gierek Fine Art.

STEVE LAUTERMILCH is a poet and photographer living in North Carolina. Recent photos have appeared as covers or as internal images in *CrossCurrents*, *North Carolina Conversations*, *Off the Coast*, and *All the Verbs of Knowing*. Recent poems have appeared or are forthcoming in *Prairie Schooner*, *Southern Poetry Review*, and *CrossCurrents*. *Rim*, a chapbook of poems, won the Sow's Ear Poetry Press competition and was recently published.

ERICA LEHRER is a Houston-based poet, journalist, fiction writer, and former practicing attorney. Her writing has appeared in national and regional publications.

ALEXANDER SHUNDI'S work is in numerous collections through the U.S. and Europe and is represented by Joseph Gierek Fine Art in Tulsa, Oklahoma.

ANNE THOMPSON, who died in 2004, was a widely recognized photographer, in addition to her work as Court Administrator for the city of Tulsa.

AMY BLOOM, judge for *Nimrod*'s 2011 Katherine Anne Porter Prize for Fiction, is the author most recently of the novel *Away* (2007) and the collection of short fiction *Where the God of Love Hangs Out* (2009). Other collections of short fiction include *Come to Me* (1993) and *A Blind Man Can See How Much I Love You* (2000). Bloom's first novel, *Love Invents Us*, was a National Book Award finalist. She has also been a nominee for the National Book Critics Circle Award for Fiction. Author also of a psychology textbook, screenplays, teleplays and television shows, she has published in *The New Yorker*, *Best American Short Stories*, *Story*, *Antaeus*, *The O. Henry Awards*, and numerous anthologies here and abroad. She taught at Yale University for ten years and is now Wesleyan University's Writer-in-Residence.

LINDA PASTAN, judge for *Nimrod*'s 2011 Pablo Neruda Prize for Poetry, has published thirteen books of poetry since 1971, including *Aspects of Eve* (1975), *The Five Stages of Grief* (1978), *Waiting For My Life* (1981), *Queen of a Rainy Country* (1986), and mostly recently, *Traveling Light* (2011). Noted for her "unfailing mastery of her medium" (*New York Times)*, she has been honored with the Dylan Thomas Award, the The Alice Fay di Castagnola Award given by the Poetry Society of America, the Bess Hokin Prize given by *Poetry Magazine*, the 1986 Maurice English Poetry Award. From 1991 to 1995 she served as the Poet Laureate of Maryland. Linda has been a contributor to *Nimrod* many times, the first time in 1968.

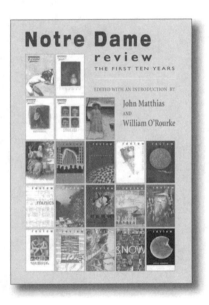

Hawai'i Pacific Review

An annual literary magazine publishing
outstanding poetry, fiction, and personal essays
by authors from Hawai'i, the mainland,
and around the world.

Individual subscriptions
$8.95 for current issue • $16.00 for two issues
$22.00 for three issues

Institutional subscriptions
$10.00 for current issue • $18.00 for two issues
$25.00 for three issues

Best of the Decade, 1986-1996 (double issue)
$10.00

Best of the Decade, 1997-2007 (double issue)
$10.00

All other back issues
$5.00

Manuscripts accepted
September 1 through December 31

Patrice Wilson, Ph.D., Editor
Hawai'i Pacific Review
Hawai'i Pacific University
1060 Bishop Street, LB7
Honolulu, Hawai'i 96813
E-mail: hpreview@hpu.edu
Web site: www.hpu.edu